THE SPORTING WORD

THE
SPORTING
WORD

**compiled by
Desmond Lynam
and David Teasdale**

ILLUSTRATIONS BY CLAUDIO MUÑOZ

BBC BOOKS

Published by BBC Books,
a division of BBC Enterprises Limited,
Woodlands, 80 Wood Lane, London W12 0TT

First published 1994
Individual quotes © the contributors
This collection © Desmond Lynam and David Teasdale

Illustrations © Claudio Muñoz

ISBN 0 563 36971 X

Set by Phoenix Photosetting, Chatham, Kent
Printed and bound in Great Britain by Clays Ltd, St Ives plc
Jacket printed by Belmont Press Ltd, Northampton

Contents

Acknowledgements

The sheer hard grind (sorry, the delightful creative experience) of any book means there are always lots of people to thank. There's all those we have quoted, for a start. Perhaps, their inclusion here is itself an acknowledgement. We shall narrow the main list down to our families, who have much already to put up with, and our colleagues. In particular, much valuable research work was done by Ceri Teasdale (often, with good grace) and by Cathy Shiells of the Coverwood Group. Finally, many thanks to our Editors Heather Holden-Brown and Julian Flanders. We did not always agree, but sometimes they were right. Julian could also be a little slow with the biscuits and sandwiches and even slower in following the Corporation internal guidelines on Encouraging Your Authors. Still, we had some fun, and exchanged some Sporting (and other) Words. We hope all who helped us are happy with the finished product. In the end, we must take all the blame.

Foreword

The language of sport is the language of war, love, politics, religion, business and of life itself. Sport also has its own unique dialect, which includes sign and body language that everybody understands. Its goals are recognized universally. Sport is about commitment and compassion, pressure and participation, highs and lows and the everyday.

Sport provides role models and examples to inspire, and deter, and these are some of the most powerful parables of modern life – and through the medium of television in particular they reach the far corners of the globe, with force and immediacy. The sporting words that capture and describe those parables are the subject of this book.

We have based this collection of quotations on two main criteria. First, of course, they have been said or written, somewhere. Many are newly published (including a number from our personal experience), some derive from the collective minds and vaults of the BBC. Second, they are the best quotations, in our opinion, in terms of aptness, interest, historical value or sheer fun. They best illustrate, or they best exemplify, the various features of the sporting world. The quotes are collected here by feature, or topic (e.g. rather than by individual sport) better to present a word picture of the many facets of the sporting life and history. This also makes it easier to find the particular quote you need for a particular occasion, for example, the after dinner address (like Des on the cover), the sales conference, the best man's speech and so on. Sometimes it may help to cross refer to find the right quote. The chapters on 'Business and Money' and 'Sponsorship', for example, have much in common.

We have drawn upon newspaper reports, magazines, books, live action, interviews and statements from around the world. Most stem from sport itself, but not all. We found in our trawls that many quotes which illuminate corners of the sporting pitch come from elsewhere. Take, for example, F. Scott Fitzgerald's description of Gatsby: 'One of those men who reach such an acute limited excellence at twenty-one that everything afterward savours of anti–climax.' Those words will strike a chord with coaches, competitors and parents across the sporting world. And has anyone expressed self-motivation better than Eleanor Roosevelt: 'No one can make you feel inferior without your consent'? So, in each section we have included quotations from out-side sport which are relevant and helpful.

Please enjoy this collection. We hope these quotes add to the knowledge and understanding of sport, and sporting endeavour, and their place in our society. They speak of fun and adventure, as well as toil and tribulation. Such is the language of sport, which is for many of us the best of life.

About Sport

If all the year were playing holidays
To sport would be as tedious as to work.
Prince Hal in SHAKESPEARE, *Henry IV, Part i*, 1598

Sport at the top level is about absolute truth.
CHRIS BRASHER, British athlete and journalist

Sport is a University of life.
LUCINDA GREEN, British Olympic three-day event rider

Sport was born of man's highest ideals and has been around for 33
centuries, which is longer than any other religion, culture or sub-
culture; it must be defended and harnessed for its values.
RON PICKERING (1930–91), British athletics coach and BBC
commentator

We who encourage sport cannot encourage it as something that is
good for you, just as it wouldn't do for us to say, listen to music
because it does you good. Rather, we must encourage it as fun, which
it is.
SIR ROGER BANNISTER, British athlete (the first four-minute-miler)
and former Chairman of the Sports Council, *New York Times*, 1979

Sport is drama without the script.
COE, TEASDALE, WICKHAM, *More Than a Game*, 1992

I think we have undervalued sport and the place it has in our national
life. . . . You watch the morale rise in any sport when we get a good
team. People like sport and they enjoy it. It is part of our natural psychology.
Prime Minister JOHN MAJOR, August 1993

Sport, which still keeps the flag of idealism flying, is perhaps the most saving grace in the world at the moment, with its spirit of rules kept, and regard for the adversary, whether the fight is going for or against. When if ever, the spirit of sport, which is the spirit of fair play, reigns over international affairs, the cat force, which rules there now, will slink away, and human life emerge for the first time from the jungle.
JOHN GALSWORTHY (1867–1933), English novelist and playwright, as quoted frequently by International Olympic Committee President Avery Brundage (1887–1975)

The game is about glory. It is about doing things in style, with a flourish, about going out and beating the other lot, not waiting for them to die of boredom.
DANNY BLANCHFLOWER (1926–93), Tottenham Hotspur and Northern Ireland footballer

Sport that wrinkled Care derides,
And Laughter holding both his sides,
Come, and trip it as ye go
On the light fantastic toe,
And in thy right hand lead with thee
The mountain nymph, sweet Liberty.
JOHN MILTON (1608–74), English poet, *L'Allegro*, 1632

Sport is recreation, it is a pastime or diversion, it is play, it is action for amusement, it is free, spontaneous and joyous – it is the opposite of work.
International Olympic Committee President AVERY BRUNDAGE (1887–1975), in opening address to 58th Session of the IOC, Athens, 16 June 1961

Here ruining people is considered sport.
VINCENT FOSTER, Deputy Legal Counsel to US President Clinton, in suicide note, July 1993

Administration

Most of the ILTF [International Lawn Tennis Federation] are idiots – a bunch of antiquated, unresponsive, self-perpetuating septuagenarians.
ARTHUR ASHE (1943–93), US tennis player, 1974

Cricket is governed by grey men who seem to want it to remain as drab and uninteresting as possible. For me cricket is the one sport which above all others is so full of hidden excitement. Any moves to highlight that ... have to be good moves. I do not want this game to fade away into the mists of nostalgia. ... My main hope for the future is that cricket is not allowed to remain in the control of guys who are living in the past.
VIVIAN RICHARDS, West Indian cricketer, in *Hitting Across the Line*, 1991

It is tragic that so much effort goes into athletics and yet the lack of inspired administration remains an insult to the aspirations of the young. Like others, I am going to emigrate wishing I could have helped the sport in my own country.
LYNN DAVIES, Welsh Olympic long jump champion, 1973

A man is known by the company he organizes.
AMBROSE BIERCE (1842–1914), American writer

95 per cent of it is down to ego.
RICK WRIGHT, Chairman of Cardiff City, on owning a football club, 1991

The authorities are in the business of making money. ... They're promoting a sport; they want to sell tickets; they want to sell TV time; they want to sell commercial sponsorship. And they can't do that if there's this image that athletes are not clean, ideal people that the world would like to perceive them as.
PAT CONNOLLY, US athletics coach, 1992

We have to remain the English bulldog SAS club. We have to sustain ourselves by sheer power and the attitude that we will kick ass. We are an academy. We find gems and turn them into finished articles.
SAM HAMMAM, Chairman of Wimbledon FC, 1992

There are people who think I shouldn't be team captain. There are people who think the Queen shouldn't be the Queen. It's something we both have to live with.
LINFORD CHRISTIE, British Olympic captain, 1992

Great, that's the Italian city with the guys in the boats, right?
MURAD MOHAMMAD, boxing promoter, on the possibility of a fight in Venezuela, 1992

The latter-day equivalent of the slave trade.
JIM JANSSEN VAN REAY, Chairman of FIFPPO (International trade union for professional footballers), on European transfer system

I must be mad. In no way is it a business venture. It has to be from the heart.
LIONEL PICKERING, Chairman of Derby County, on his £10 million spend for the club, 1993

From the beginning I believed that staying the course was what counted. I outlast the bastards. The sheer process of attrition wears the others down. That was my belief then. It still is now.
HARRISON FORD, actor, on early clashes with film directors/producers indifferent to performance standards, 1993

When you own a National Football League team, it's like a valuable painting. It's unique and priceless. This was a challenge that I had to meet in an aggressive way.
JERRY JONES, owner of Dallas Cowboys, August 1993

Side-saddle habit should be of a restrained hue with long black boots. The bowler hat should be a safety bowler and be worn with an unwrinkled veil. A silk hat is traditionally only correct if worn after midday at shows of county standard and upwards, and never for pre-liminary judging.
Guidelines in the *Side-saddle Association Handbook*, 1992

So far, I have had a brooch removed and told a competitor to take off her cardigan. Only plain knitted woollens are allowed. ... Earrings can be studs or clip-ons, but no danglers. ... You can wear a plain gold chain, but we don't want people flaunting their diamonds and pearls.
Junior Vice President in charge of uniform inspection at English Women's National Bowling Championships, Royal Leamington Spa, August 1993

It is hard to tell where MCC ends and the Church of England begins.
J. B. PRIESTLEY (1894–1984), British novelist, Poet Laureate, article in *New Statesman*, 1962

I could go to any county committee room if I wanted to see that.
FRED TRUEMAN, English cricketer and commentator, explaining why he had not been to see the classic Spielberg dinosaur film, *Jurassic Park*, 1993

He knows nothing and he thinks he knows everything. That points clearly to a political career.
GEORGE BERNARD SHAW (1856–1950), Irish dramatist, in *Major Barbara*, 1905

You don't get given power, you have to take it.
RICK PARRY, Chief Executive of FA Premier League, 1993

Administratively, Britain lost their authority, which was long taken for granted, not because of errors but because other nations, especially Latins, realised the scope of power, and once they gained it were reluctant to relinquish it.

It is a fact that the British structure tends to prevent anyone coming through [internationally], but there will be a swing. The trouble is that the British today do not have enough team spirit [in committee]. You have to prepare yourself long in advance for election. You need national presidents who are chairmen of the executive board day by day.
SEPP BLATTER, FIFA General Secretary, commenting on Britain's loss of influence in world soccer administration, December 1993

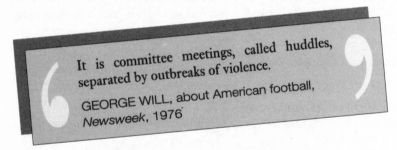

It is committee meetings, called huddles, separated by outbreaks of violence.
GEORGE WILL, about American football, *Newsweek*, 1976

Sport has not always made its case to the best of its ability. The best example is the huge discrepancy between the Arts Council grant and the Sports Council grant. We have tended not to play the political game.
SEBASTIAN COE, Vice Chairman of the Sports Council, 1986

3

After the Match

It's not the end of the world. My dog will still lick my face whether I win or lose.
MATT BIONDI, US swimmer, after losing his Olympic 100 metre freestyle title, 1992

Once again we got a good kick up the backside. Maybe it's the shot in the arm we needed.
ALLAN BORDER, Australian Test cricket captain, after losing to South Africa by 9 wickets in the 1992 World Cup

How did I feel when I won? Numb. Of course you know precisely how you're supposed to feel, but when you've spent ten years working for something that is over in a split second, your mind just goes blank. Perhaps the experience was wasted on me, because it was all over so quickly. I was shell shocked. I still feel strange. It hasn't sunk in even yet.
CHRIS BOARDMAN reflecting on his cycling gold medal at the Barcelona Olympic Games, December 1992

I feel as if I've got a monkey off my back. In fact, I feel as if I've got a whole troupe of monkeys off my back.
NICK PRICE, Zimbabwean golfer, after winning his first major, the US PGA, 1992

Nothing, apart maybe from sex, has ever given me the thrill that did.
IAN STARK, three day eventer, after Olympic cross-country ride on Murphy Himself, 1992

It was worth getting your knickers wet for.
JENNY CARDWELL, England women's hockey manager, after win in the rain over Olympic champions Spain, 1992

This has got to be the greatest day of my life. It's taken a long time, it's been a slow process and I'm clean. I had to do this for the morale of the team.
LINFORD CHRISTIE, British athlete, after winning Olympic 100 metre gold medal, 1992

I'd like to be a superhero all my life but today my cape fell off.
MATT BIONDI, US swimmer, after missing a medal in the Olympic 100 metre freestyle, 1992

Sure, it was important to me, but to who else? The sun will be out tomorrow and the stars and the moon will be out tonight. It was only a race.
MICHAEL JOHNSON, US sprinter, after losing 200 metre semi-final when favourite, Olympic Games, 1992

And we were lucky to get nil.
Member of Scottish rugby team beaten 44–0 by South Africa, 1952

My biggest player was not as big as their smallest.
PETER STUBBE, Thailand soccer coach, on their 4–0 loss to Saudi Arabia, 1993

It was a wedding, a funeral, every emotion you can ever feel; a vindication of everything this country has been through for the last fifty years.
DONN NIELSEN, assistant coach to Lithuanian basketball team, after beating Unified Team to win Olympic bronze medal, 1992

Until they got their fourth goal, we were outplaying them.
BERNIE COTTON, Britain's hockey manager, after 6–0 defeat by Australia in Barcelona Olympic Games, 1992

We've not come here to entertain. We've come to win.
Footballer CARLTON PALMER, after England's 0–0 draw with
France, Euro '92

I feel I have been betrayed by young brats.
PIERRE BERBIZIER, French rugby union coach, after losing to
Argentina, 1993

My feet could do with a 10 000 mile service.
FFYONA CAMPBELL, trans-Africa walker, September 1993

We did spend a week at Lourdes.
GERRY MURPHY, Ireland rugby coach, after his side's surprise win
over England, 1993

I'm just off for a quiet pint. Followed by fifteen noisy ones.
GARETH CHILCOTT, Bath (and England) rugby union player, after
last game for the club, 1993

Against Sport

Games are the last resort of those that do not know how to be idle.
ROBERT LYND (1879–1949), Anglo-Irish essayist/journalist

The greatest dread of all, the dread of games.
JOHN BETJEMAN (1906–84), Poet Laureate

Like every instrument man has invented, sport can be used for good and evil purposes. Used badly, it can encourage personal vanity and group vanity, greedy desire for victory, and even hatred for rivals, an intolerant esprit de corps and contempt for people who are beyond an arbitrary selected pale.
ALDOUS HUXLEY (1894–1963), English novelist

I hate sports as rabidly as a person who likes sports hates common sense.
H. L. MENCKEN (1880–1956), US journalist

Sport is hard work for which you do not get paid.
IRVIN S. COBB (1876–1944), US writer

Games are for people who can neither read nor think.
GEORGE BERNARD SHAW (1856–1950), Irish dramatist

Sport is an unfailing cause of ill-will.
GEORGE ORWELL (1903–50), English novelist

Detested sport,
That owes its pleasures to another's pain.
WILLIAM COWPER (1731–1800), English poet, *The Winter Evening*

Wild animals never kill for sport. Man is the only one to whom the torture and death of his fellow creatures is amusing in itself.
J. A. FROUDE (1818–94), English historian, *Oceana*, 1886

5

Age

It's a funny old world. It's a lucky man who gets out of it alive.
W. C. FIELDS (1879–1946), US humorist

What is an adult? A child blown up by age.
SIMONE DE BEAUVOIR (1908–86), French novelist and feminist

Youth is a period of missed opportunities.
CYRIL CONNOLLY (1903–74), British critic

Everyone has talent at 25. The difficulty is to have it at 50.
EDGAR DEGAS (1834–1917), French painter/sculptor

First, your legs go. Then you lose your reflexes. Then you lose your friends.
WILLIE PEP, US boxer, World featherweight champion, 1942–48, 1949–50

I don't know that my behaviour has improved that much with age. They just found somebody worse.
JIMMY CONNORS, US tennis player, 1984

Ask Nureyev to stop dancing, ask Sinatra to stop singing, then you can ask me to stop playing tennis.
BILLIE JEAN KING, US tennis player, 1983

We do not stop playing because we are old; we grow old because we stop playing.
ANON

Age is jocund; it makes sport for death.
Proverb

My chief regret for the advance of life is that the infirmities of age compel me to renounce the enjoyment of field sports.
Prime Minister ROBERT WALPOLE (1676–1745)

It is not an old people's game because you have to be fit to play it.
EILEEN GOODE, President of English Women's Bowling, August 1993

Bowls is a young man's game that old men can play.
DAVID BRYANT, English lawn bowler, winner of the world title in 1980, fourteen years after his previous victory

The problem now is that when you have an indifferent game at 37 they say that the legs are going. They don't take into consideration that you might just be having an off day, carrying an injury or struggling with a cold. When it happens to a 20-year-old it's called inexperience!
RAY WILKINS, English footballer, December 1993

A lady of a certain age, which means
Certainly aged.
LORD BYRON (1788–1824), English poet, *Don Juan*, 1819

A man is only as old as the woman he feels.
GROUCHO MARX (1895–1977), US humorist

I no count the years. Men may steal my chickens, men may steal my sheep. But no man may steal my age.
MIRUTS YIFTER, Ethiopian double Olympic gold medallist

I'll never make the mistake of being 70 again. . . . Charles de Gaulle is older than me, and he's running a country.
CASEY STENGEL (1891–1975), New York Yankees manager, on being sacked for being too old

The tragedy of old age is not that one is old, but that one is young.
MARK TWAIN (1835–1910), US writer and wit

Age is not any indication of fitness.
SEBASTIAN COE, British athlete, 1986

The legend is now stretching the reality and it's beginning to hurt. Desert Orchid won again at Sandown yesterday; great warm waves swept over the Surrey hillside but the signs of age were there.
BROUGH SCOTT, racing commentator, 1991

I know I am not the player I was day in, day out, and that bothers me every day of my life. .... The trouble is that when I go home my interest wanes. Nowadays, I have to put in more time for less results, which is hard to accept. It is also hard to accept losing to people there was once no way of losing to.
JOHN McENROE, US tennis player, 1991

Twenty years ago, at my age, I would probably have been retired. By that time I would certainly have been looking at the rest of my life and wondering what to do for a living. But there have been big changes in the sport and I am able to be a full time athlete. It is my profession and to maintain my standard of living I have to work harder as I get older.
GREG FOSTER after winning the World championship 110 metre hurdles for the third successive time, Tokyo, 31 August 1991

To be told you are too old at 35 by a man of 39 batting better than at any time in his career gives the impression it's not the real reason.
DAVID GOWER, English cricketer, 1992 (the reference is to the then England captain, Graham Gooch)

I consider myself very fortunate to have had the best seasons of my career when most people are finishing. I have become a steadier player and still scored at a good rate. If I can do that again in this, my fortieth year, it would be great. Everything else is a bonus.
GRAHAM GOOCH, English cricketer, April 1993

It's not worth it any more. My hips go, my knees get too sore, my back stiffens up and I can't bend.
JIMMY CONNORS, US tennis player, after losing at Wimbledon in first round, 1992

New guys have been telling me I was too old. But I've been getting faster as the years go by. Age is just in the mind.
LINFORD CHRISTIE, British athlete, after winning Olympic 100 metre gold medal, 1992

I know I could still make a decent living from tennis, but that's not why I play.

If I had one wish it would be that I enjoyed it more at the time.
JOHN McENROE, US tennis player, 1993

It's hell being 40.
JIMMY CONNORS, US tennis player, 1992

Who knows how long I can go on for? Maybe, after the next fall. I feel fit enough. But I get a lot of aches and pains and I'm not as supple as I was.
WILLIE CARSON, English jockey, on turning 50, 1993

I need a new pair of glasses every two months, my eyesight is going that quickly. I just hope these glasses will last until Saturday and I can take a frame off Hendry.
CLIFF WILSON, Welsh snooker player aged 58, 1993

You're as old as you need to be. As long as you're fit enough, you're young enough.
JEFF PROBYN, England rugby union player, January 1993

If you look back, you fall downstairs.
RUDOLF NUREYEV (1939–93), Russian ballet dancer

The older you are, the harder you have to practise.
KEITH FLETCHER, England cricket manager, 1993

It's not how old you are, it's how you're old.
BRIAN BLESSED, actor, contemplating an Everest ascent at 57 (to make him the oldest to reach the summit), February 1993

At my age, to win and have a pulse on the same day is pretty good.
PAUL NEWMAN, US actor, on his car racing passion aged 68, February 1993

Some of the players were put aside because they were in their thirties but it doesn't mean they won't return.
GUY LAPORTE, French Rugby Union Chairman, commenting on French squad to tour South Africa, May 1993

By the time I was 16 I was a has been.
MARY DECKER, US athlete

Today I had a bad day. Age is not why I lost, but it certainly makes things more difficult to get going when you're older and things don't quite go your way.
MARTINA NAVRATILOVA, US tennis player, after losing Wimbledon tennis semi-final v. Novotna, 1993

The danger now is that there are too many alternatives in my life. I have to keep telling myself: yes, it does matter; no, you can't afford to lose.
DAVID MOORCROFT, British athlete, on his attempts to become the first over-40 to run a four-minute mile, 1993

I wish them well. Whether they do it depends on how well they've kept in training. Changes in the lungs and heart become more pronounced at that age.
SIR ROGER BANNISTER, British athlete, commenting on those attempts, 1993

The saddest thing about age is the day you hear that another lifelong chum has gone. Those are bad days. There are not many left of my vintage now.
DENIS COMPTON, English cricketer, May 1993

No daddy, you're too old. Please don't do it.
BLANE McGUIGAN, 10-year-old son of former world featherweight champion Barry, 32, who turned down offers of a comeback, 1993

When I was 10, all I ever dreamed of was playing at Wimbledon, with the greats, and having my ears pierced.
TRACEY AUSTIN, US tennis player, 1992

Ages is a state of mind. If you're producing the goods, you're producing the goods.... It bugs me when people witter on about age.... Experience is a huge compensation in a game like cricket, particularly for a spin bowler.
JOHN EMBUREY, English cricketer, January 1994

Towering is the confidence of 21.
DR SAMUEL JOHNSON (1709–84), English lexicographer

The worst thing about life is the number of horses and dogs you outlive.
LORD OAKSEY, racing commentator, interviewed on *Desert Island Discs*, 1993

Hope I die before I get old.
THE WHO, *My Generation* (words by Pete Townshend), 1965

It's all right letting yourself go, as long as you can let yourself back.
MICK JAGGER, rock musician, 1982

Youth, which is forgiven everything, forgives itself nothing; age, which forgives itself everything, is forgiven nothing.

It's all the young can do for the old, to shock them and keep them up-to-date.
GEORGE BERNARD SHAW (1856–1950), Irish dramatist

When I grow up, I want to be a little boy.
JOSEPH HELLER, US writer, *Something Happened*, 1974

6

Amateurs

Professionals built the *Titanic*, amateurs built the Ark.
ANON

Amateur: one who plays games for the love of the thing. Unlike the professional, he receives no salary, and is contented with presents of clothes, clubs, racquets, cigarettes, cups, cheques, hotel expenses, fares and so on.
J. B. MORTON (1893–1979), English author and journalist, writing under the name of 'Beachcomber', 1974

The British public has always had an unerring taste for the ungifted amateurs.
JOHN OSBORNE, English playwright, 1957

There are no amateurs any more. To be good a skier must literally devote from four to six years of his life to the sport. You don't have time for school, or a job, and you must travel the world. That's hard to do without compensation.
JEAN-CLAUDE KILLY, French skier, 1972

My ambition is to have a British ski team picked on ability alone, not one that can afford to pay for the honour themselves.
ROBIN BAILEY, British ski team manager, 1974

Let's be honest – a proper definition of an amateur today is one who accepts cash, not cheques.
JACK KELLY JNR, US Olympic Committee, 1983

Any rugby union player worth his salt in France who does not accept payment is considered a fool and a rare one at that.
CHRIS LAIDLAW, New Zealand rugby union player, 1974

Rugby can be a very violent game if there is £1000 per man riding on the result.
BOB WEIGHILL, Secretary of the Rugby Football Union, 1983

The only real amateur is one who pays his own expenses.
VIVIAN JENKINS, Welsh rugby union player, later sportswriter

When you are on one side of the world getting your ribs kicked in for your country, the gas bills are still coming in at home.
GARETH EDWARDS, Welsh rugby union player, c. 1980

The amateur has an unalienable right to play like a pillock.
DICK GREENWOOD, rugby union coach, 1985

In England you are expected to do it all for good old Blighty.
MIKE TEAGUE, English rugby union player, 1991

I have always believed that no one should ever receive money for actually playing rugby ... it would ruin the game itself and the whole structure of rugby in Britain.
BILL BEAUMONT, English rugby union player and commentator, *Thanks to Rugby*, 1982

Sometime we will be paid for playing rugby, but it can only be at international level. There's just not the money lower down.
MICHAEL LYNAGH, Australian rugby union player, 1993

I've never advocated being paid for playing and even now, as a professional, it's pride in performance and not money that motivates me on the field. There is far more money in rugby union than league, but only in the league does any of it go to the players. But top rugby union players have to commit themselves – at the top it's 90 per cent preparation and only 10 per cent participation. And we all have families to support and futures to think about.
JONATHAN DAVIES, star of rugby union and rugby league, 1992

I'm still an amateur, of course, but I became rugby's first millionaire five years ago.
DAVID CAMPESE, Australian rugby union player, 1991

We are preparing like top Olympic athletes and pro footballers, where is it all leading? The way it's going we'll be professionals. I didn't come into the game for that.
DICK BEST, England rugby union coach, January 1993

Amateurism in athletics is dead. It has been a ghost of its original self for years.
GEOFF CAPES, British athlete, 1981

The amateur system is an insult to my ego and intelligence. It's insulting to me to have to exist like this. People in the sport feel like they are doing something illegal just to survive.
ED MOSES, US athlete, 1981

We have to cut out all this amateur crap. It's phoney. We have to be openly professional, money on the table where everyone can see it.
CARL LEWIS, US athlete, 1988

They think we just have to run, and will show, whatever they offer us. It's 99 per cent a business venture.
LEROY BURRELL, US athlete, explaining his absence from US Championships in 1991

The brown envelope system wasn't one that most of us were happy with. It forced people to act dishonestly – according to the strict rules then of the sport.
SEBASTIAN COE, British athlete, reflecting in 1992 on his early days in athletics (in the late 1970s)

There was, and is, no greater thrill than pulling on my country's vest. That thrill has not diminished. But to get to that top level, and to stay there for fourteen years, I had to commit myself to the sport. That was not compatible with advancing a normal career.
SEBASTIAN COE, 1992

The only amateurs here are the organizers.
East German official at Lake Placid Winter Olympic Games, 1980

Give the labourer his wage before his perspiration be dry.
MUHAMMAD (*c.* AD 570–632), prophet

Pray God that no professional will ever captain Yorkshire.
LORD HAWKE (1860–1938), when President of Yorkshire County Cricket Club

W. G. Grace: the best paid amateur of all time.
ANON

The passing of the amateur captain was one of the worst things that has ever happened to cricket.
BRIAN CLOSE, English cricketer, 1993

Money is the most corroding influence . . . it changes the whole perspective in sport and brings in a completely new range of motives and considerations.
HRH DUKE OF EDINBURGH, 1986

England are flogging them to death. Players are physically and mentally knackered. It's supposed to be an amateur game yet amateur principles are going out of the window. Of course, this England team, in terms of fitness, is unrecognizable to the 1980 Grand Slam team, but it is at great cost to the clubs who have to pick up the pieces.
BARRIE CORLESS, Northampton rugby union coach, 1993

It's fantastic to play for your country, but part of the buzz is this amateur thing. This week, I've been in my office, Rory Underwood has been flying planes for the RAF, Wade Dooley has been on the beat in Blackpool. Then, halfway through the week, we leave our offices saying, see you lads, got to prepare for the match on Saturday.
ROB ANDREW, English rugby union player, before playing for England against France, January 1993

Lewis and Leroy Burrell got five times as much as Dennis [Mitchell] and he won the race. Look, you've got to change things and I'm sure it's going to get nastier before it gets clean.
TONY CAMPBELL, coach/agent, on 1992 Grand Prix Final

I can't see too many players leaving Wales in the future. They are getting looked after better now, and from the rumours I hear, even the lower clubs are paying quite good wages. I've no regrets. My main consideration was providing for my family and league was the only option I had, but I doubt if I would be tempted now.
JONATHAN DAVIES, star of rugby union and rugby league, January 1993

In Scotland we couldn't become more professional because we don't have the population to support a professional game. We only have 12 000 players in a population of 5 million . . . I doubt if rugby union in Britain could ever support professional playing staffs.
IAN McGEECHAN, Scotland and British Lions rugby union coach, January 1993

I believed that in an amateur game, if I was not having fun, what was I doing there?
STUART BARNES, English rugby union player, 1993

Rugby is facing its biggest dilemma ever. The expansion of the World Cup between 1987 and 1991, in sponsorship and spectator interest, has led to increased demands by administrators, the game and players. The administrators ARE moving towards compensating players, but the compensation is not sufficient. There is no doubt in my mind that, within five to seven years, rugby union will be a professional game. Whether it could sustain itself, at club level, is another matter. Almost certainly not in Scotland.
GAVIN HASTINGS, Scotland and British Lions captain, December 1993

I have been accused of being an elitist and I am. I believe we are lucky to be involved in this [rugby] freemasonry and, if that's elitist, then I accept it.
DUDLEY WOOD, Secretary of the Rugby Football Union, November 1993

We believe the game is better for being a recreation, a diversion for those pursuing their careers in other fields, and nothing we see in professional sport persuades us that it is time to surrender.
DUDLEY WOOD, Secretary of the Rugby Football Union, in letter to *The Times*, 23 December 1993

How many times do I have to tell you, we don't want any amateurs here!
LEW GRADE, Head of ITV, when told that they had a deal with the Amateur Athletic Association for track and field coverage in preference to the BBC, 1964

The amateur code, coming to us from antiquity, contributed to and strengthened by the noblest aspirations of great men of each generation, embraces the highest moral laws. No philosophy, no religion, preaches loftier sentiments.
AVERY BRUNDAGE (1887–1975), International Olympic Committee President, 1952

We used to say, yes, we are amateurs, students or servicemen, but of course we were in fact professionals . . . [sport] was our living.
VLADIMIR PILGUY, Russian Olympian, 1992

It didn't worry us a fig that amateurs came out of a different gate than us.
DENIS COMPTON, English cricketer, 1993

If someone can send me a new bicycle, I would be grateful.
HUANG ZHIHONG, Chinese world champion woman shotputter, still waiting for her Mercedes won in Stuttgart 1993 and reflecting on student poverty, at Loughborough University, 19 October 1993

Rugby is still meant to be an amateur game and you should be able to play in Hong Kong Sevens or anywhere else if you want to. Yet when you look at this season's fixtures there is no time to play outside the leagues. It's just ridiculous. I think a variety of games is desirable. It's a shame there are no holes left in the fixture list.
WILL CARLING, England rugby union captain, October 1993

There's no money in rugby, unless you are the captain.
JEFF PROBYN, England rugby union player, December 1993

This is hard work for nothing. I think it is the last time we will be running for free.
CARL LEWIS, US athlete, August 1993

If I was paid, I might not tell him what I think. Now I can tell him anything I want.
TOM TELLEZ, coach to Carl Lewis, 1993

I'm a company, he's a company. The idea is for my company to out-perform his company.
CARL LEWIS, US athlete, on his race with Linford Christie, before the two companies banked £100 000 each, at Gateshead, 1993

We've moved on from the days when we used to have to buy all of our kit and stay in youth hostels – we now get reasonable deals from hotels, and kit sponsorship. But the World Cup next year will cost each player between £750 and £1000.
EMMA MITCHELL, scrum half to England women's rugby union team, December 1993

'Art for art's sake' means in practice: 'Success for money's sake'. Great art is never produced for its own sake. It is too difficult to be worth the effort.
GEORGE BERNARD SHAW (1856–1950), Irish dramatist, 1910

Some people get petrol money, but I get a car.
KEVIN DUNN, English rugby union player, 1993

Let's face it, this is a semi-professional sport. You are living in cloud cuckoo land if you don't accept that you are going to lose players if you are relegated.
MARK EVANS, Saracens rugby union coach, 1993

We assumed he had been found a job in the capital. It was difficult to picture Nigel as a city Eurobond dealer, but imagine the surprise at Gloucester when we discovered he had been found a job as a postman – in Cirencester.
KEITH RICHARDSON, Gloucester rugby union coach, on Nigel Scrivens joining London Welsh, 1993

No person is allowed directly or indirectly to receive payment, benefit or other material reward or to accept the promise of future payment, benefit or other material reward for taking part in the game.
Byelaw 4, International Rugby Football Board rules

The biggest [problem] is the strain that exists between the amateur principles, which the IRFB's written constitution purports to uphold, and their flagrant and widespread abuse in practice.
GERALD DAVIES, former Wales and British Lions rugby union player, *The Times*, 31 December 1993

The IRFB itself is no longer of the [amateur] faith. Where the spirit was once charitable, it is now moved by market forces.
GERALD DAVIES, 31 December 1993

Anyone good enough to win one already has one.
MICHAEL JOHNSON, US sprinter (and eventual winner of 400 metre world title), on the prize of a £20 000 Mercedes for the winners at the World Athletics Championships, 1993

7

Animals

There is a passion for hunting, something deeply implanted in the human breast.
CHARLES DICKENS (1812–70), English novelist, *Oliver Twist*, 1837

My hoarse sounding horn
Invites thee to the chase, the sport of kings;
Image of war, without its guilt.
WILLIAM SOMERVILLE (1675–1742), English poet, *The Chase*, 1735

When a man wantonly destroys one of the works of man, we call him a vandal. When he destroys one of the works of God, we call him a sportsman.
JOSEPH WOOD KRUTCH (1893–1970), American essayist

It used to be the sport of kings, but now horse racing is an industry and a cutthroat one at that.
HENRY CECIL, English trainer, 1991

Thoroughbreds have always been raced at two and three-years-old, but up till the 1970s they used to train on for longer. Since then, owners don't want to risk damage, or reduced value; it's such an industry now, they can't afford the risk.
LESTER PIGGOTT, English jockey, 1992

There is no secret so close as that between a rider and his horse.
ROBERT SURTEES (1803–64), English writer, *Mr Sponge's Sporting Tour*, 1853

It ar'nt that I loves the fox less, but that I loves the 'ound more.
ROBERT SURTEES, *Handley Cross*, 1843

Horses are like children; they'll learn something bad quicker than they'll learn something good.
PHILIP WALSH, writer

Generally, people who are working with animals in sport are doing so because they love them.
NICKY COE, British equestrienne, 1992

You have to get horses there without them realizing it. You can't persuade them to go through a pain barrier – like you can with people. The best horses are often lazy in a gallop. It's important they don't hurt themselves. If their lungs are hurting, the next time they will resent it. It's important they give a performance first time out.

They are a backward type of animal. They can probably only run two or three times at their peak.
HENRY CECIL, English trainer, 1991

The tragic climax of the horse's career [in the bullfight] has occurred off stage at an earlier time; when he was bought by the horse contractor for use in the bull ring.

The death of the horses in the ring is an unavoidable accident and affords pleasure to no one connected with or viewing the fight except the bull, who derives supreme satisfaction from it.

In the tragedy of the bullfight, the horse is the comic character.
ERNEST HEMINGWAY (1899–1961), US novelist, *Death in the Afternoon*, 1932

People who are involved in it feel very strongly about it. This is part of their culture and they are not going to give it up without a fight.
RAYMONDE LaLONDE, American Congressman, on cockfighting, 1992

A dog teaches a boy fidelity, perseverance and to turn round three times before lying down.
ROBERT BENCHLEY (1889–1945), US humorist and critic

If you pick up a starving dog and make him prosperous, he will not bite you; that is the principal difference between a dog and a man.
MARK TWAIN (1835–1910), US writer and wit

The English country gentleman galloping after a fox; the unspeakable in full pursuit of the uneatable.
OSCAR WILDE (1854–1900), Irish wit and playwright, in *A Woman of No Importance*, 1893

It is chiefly through the instinct to kill that man achieves intimacy with the life of nature.
LORD (SIR KENNETH) CLARK (1903–83), English art historian

A horse is dangerous at both ends and uncomfortable in the middle.
IAN FLEMING (1908–64), English novelist

You cameramen are getting my goat. Horses are very sensitive. They are not like humans. They don't understand what all the fuss is about.
HRH PRINCESS ANNE, 1973

In nature there are neither rewards nor punishments – there are consequences.
R. G. INGERSOLL (1833–99), US lawyer

English country gents often hunt birds and no one objected when Sheikh Zaid Ben Sultan, ruler of Abu Dhabi, decided to try his hand at the sport at his luxurious English mansion in the shires. What distressed neighbours was that he used a machine gun.
Newsweek magazine, 1976

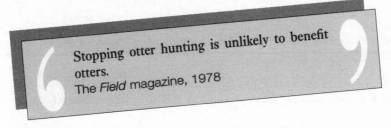

Stopping otter hunting is unlikely to benefit otters.
The *Field* magazine, 1978

The golden rule in dealing with a horse is never to approach him angrily.
XENOPHON (428–354 BC), Athenian soldier

At the Olympics I love watching almost anything that's special, as long as it doesn't have a horse in it.
DALEY THOMPSON, British athlete, 1988

The great thing is that we're both incidental to the horse, and unless we have a good horse, there's nothing either of us can do.
PETER SCUDAMORE, jockey, talking about his partnership with trainer Martin Pipe, 1992

A human who is feeling dreadful can pull himself up. A horse has a jockey urging him on. The potential for damage is enormous.
MARTIN PIPE, trainer, 1992

The public should not have a say in this, it should be left to the professionals who understand what they are looking at. Horses spend 23 hours out of 24 every day in luxury. They might get their bottoms smacked six times in their lives. I'm stressed six times a day, six days a week. When I come back to Earth, I want to be a thoroughbred in a good stable.
GRAHAM THORNER, English trainer, on the debate about the use of whips, 1992

If there's one quality I want to see in a horse, it's courage. I've also never known a really good horse that wasn't intelligent.
NIGEL MURLESS, English trainer, 1959

If he were a human being, he would be in the Olivier, Fonteyn, Pavarotti league.
JUDITH DRAPER, writing on *Milton, Super Champion*, 1992

If I have a complaint about hunting, it is that they don't kill enough foxes.
SIR NICHOLAS RIDLEY (1929–93), English politician

I'm lucky because I have an athlete between my legs.
WILLIE CARSON, English jockey, 1992

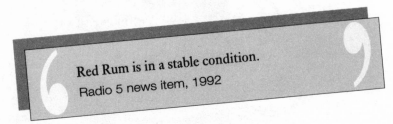

Red Rum is in a stable condition.
Radio 5 news item, 1992

I would rather a horse of mine was beaten by a neck than win by a neck with a good thrashing.
MARY REVELEY, trainer, 1992

They will never bury him. Nijinsky died on Wednesday. He now lies beneath three feet of Kentucky earth. But the memory still gallops free. The best I have ever seen.
BROUGH SCOTT, racing commentator, 1992

Animals are such agreeable friends – they ask no questions, they pass no criticisms.
GEORGE ELIOT (1819–80), English novelist

There are three faithful friends – an old wife, an old dog, and ready money.
BENJAMIN FRANKLIN (1706–90), US inventor

Histories are more full of examples of the fidelity of dogs than of friends.
ALEXANDER POPE (1688–1744), English poet

Owners don't want to hear that their horse is useless, and when I get off horses trainers are always trying to get me away from their owners in case I say too much. It might be brutal, but I always tell the truth.
WILLIE CARSON, English jockey, October 1993

I used to be a great supporter. I saw the hare beat the dogs and it was limping away from the field when a beater took a pole and beat it to death. The ones that get killed first are the luckiest.
JOE DURKIN, who has been attending the Waterloo Cup for thirty years, the last five as a protester, 1993

Shoot all the bluejays you want, if you can hit 'em, but remember it's a sin to kill a mockingbird.
HARPER LEE, *To Kill A Mockingbird*, 1960

Outside of a dog, a book is a man's best friend. Inside of a dog, it's too dark to read.
S. J. PERELMAN (1904–79), US humourist and writer

Three things I never lends – my 'oss, my wife and my name.
ROBERT SURTEES (1803–64), English writer, *Hillingdon Hall*, 1845

Tell me a man's a fox hunter, and I loves him at once.
ROBERT SURTEES, 1843

For I must go where lazy Peace
Will hide her drowsy head;
And, for the sport of kings, increase
The number of the dead.
SIR WILLIAM D'AVENANT (1606–68), English poet and playwright, *The Soldier Going to the Field*

'Well, what sort of sport has Lord – had?'
'Oh, the young Sahib shot divinely, but God was very merciful to the birds.'
G. W. E. RUSSELL (1853–1919), English politician and author, *Collections & Recollections*, 1898

Jeremy's a gentleman, he always waits for his orders. Goose more or less takes control of the situation and I have to live with it.
LUCINDA MURRAY, British equestrienne, talking about her horses, Badminton Horse Trials, 1994

A horse! A horse! My kingdom for a horse!
King Richard in SHAKESPEARE, *Richard III*, 1591

8

Background and Education

If I'd gone to Cambridge or Oxford there'd have been no limits to what I could've achieved.
GEOFFREY BOYCOTT, English cricketer, 1974

A high degree of skill and intelligence are required for croquet and therefore it's not going to attract the lower income groups.
M. B. RECKITT (1888–1979), Chairman of Croquet Association, *The Times*, 1974

I became a woman wrestler because they said it didn't need any 'O' levels.
MITZI MUELLER, US wrestler, 1974

The cricket and football fields are not merely places of exercise and amusement; they help to form some of the most valuable social qualities and manly virtues.
Royal Commission on Public Schools, 1864

Some local education authorities actually think competitive sport is bad for children. They'll be telling us next that water doesn't suit goldfish.
RICHARD TRACEY, MP, Minister for Sport, 1987

You can't hit, you can't throw but you sure can run bases. Go and work out for the track team.
High School baseball coach to US athlete LEROY BURRELL, who quoted it after breaking the 100 metres world record in June 1991

You can take a guy out of the ghetto, but you can't take the ghetto out of the guy.
VINCENT J. FULLER, US lawyer, defending US boxer Mike Tyson on rape charge, 1992

The first thing you have to be if you want to play in the top flight is an athlete. Fifteen years ago the first thing you had to be was a technician.
GRAEME SOUNESS, football manager, 1993

Seb is a Yorkshireman. So he's a complete bastard and will do well in politics.
DALEY THOMPSON, British athlete, on fellow-athlete Sebastian Coe, January 1993

The only people we would not even look at are people from Yorkshire.
SIR RANULPH FIENNES, British explorer, on staffing future expeditions, 1993

The British don't like clever people and chess is seen as a game for clever people.
NIGEL SHORT, British Chess Grand Master, 1993

> Me having no education, I had to use my brains.
> BILL SHANKLY (1913–81), football manager

A ball player's got to be kept hungry . . . that's why no boy from a nice family ever made the big leagues.
JOE DIMAGGIO, US baseball player

We ourselves don't know the makeup. We choose players who are Lebanese, the best players we can find, and to go round asking people's background would be to destroy everything we are now working towards. They are footballers, that's it.
KHALED SALAAM, Lebanese Government Head of Protocol, replying to questions about the religious background of players in the Lebanese team on their return to World Cup football, May 1993

There are those who reckon it [darts] has no place in a yuppie society. But I think they've gone overboard in cleaning it up. Darts is *about* pints, fags and blokes in cardigans.
SID WADDELL, darts commentator, 1990

All over the British Isles, men and women are giving their time to keep the soul alive, teaching the rudiments of cricket to children in the hope that, as well as a love of the game, they will be imbued with something of the philosophy of the game; its unique place in the nation's life, its nobility of spirit, its code of chivalry and respect.
GRAEME WRIGHT, former editor of *Wisden*, in *Betrayal: The Struggle for Cricket's Soul*, 1993

I went in helpless. But I came out armed and dangerous with knowledge.
DON KING, boxing promoter, on his time in prison in the 1960s

My mother made me play cricket because she didn't want me to rob white men's houses, wreck cars and smoke cannabis and cocaine.
WALTER MASEMOLA, South African black fast bowler, 1993

He's a bewtiful jumper but he will keep using great long words like corrugated iron and marmalade.
Welsh rugby union player RAY PROSSER on England's David Marques, *c*. 1956

Footballers are interested only in drinking, clothes and the size of their willies.
KARREN BRADY, Birmingham City managing director, 1993

He uses those short, sharp words, just like hooks and upper cuts. You always know what he's saying 'cause he says it very clearly. But a guy like Francis Bacon, hey, the sentences just go on and on.
MIKE TYSON, US boxer, about his reading education in gaol, March 1994

9

Body and Exercise

I've been told that I retain a lot of moisture when I eat.
PAUL GASCOIGNE, English footballer, 1993

I like long walks, especially when they are taken by people who annoy me.
FRED ALLEN (1894–1956), US humorist

MR UNIVERSE: Don't forget, Mr Carson, your body is the only home you'll ever have.

JOHNNY CARSON: Yes, my home is pretty messy. But I have a woman who comes in once a week.
From Johnny Carson's US tv Chat Show

That's not exercise, that's flagellation.
NOEL COWARD (1899–1973), English actor, dramatist and composer, on squash

Exercise is bunk. If you are healthy, you don't need it, if you are sick, you shouldn't take it.
HENRY FORD (1863–1947), US industrialist

Whenever I feel like exercise I lie down until the feeling passes.
ROBERT M. HUTCHINS (1899–1977), American educator/ writer

I get my exercise acting as a pallbearer to my friends who exercise.
CHAUNCEY DEPEW (1834–1928), USA Republican politician

Running races should be absolutely forbidden to men over 27 years of age. Between 30 and 40 a man may indulge in running at a moderate pace for exercise, but not in races. Men over 60 years of age should never run at all for anything, not even to catch a train.
Physical Efficiency magazine, 1906

The body when over-laboured becomes heavy and jaded; but it is exercise alone that supports the spirits, and keeps the mind in vigour.

Exercise and temperance can preserve something of our early strength even in old age.
CICERO (106–43 BC), Roman statesman and writer

Two things only the people anxiously desire, bread and the circus games.
JUVENAL (AD 60–130), Roman lawyer and satirist

To win back my youth there is nothing I won't do – except take exercise, get up early, and be a useful member of the community.
OSCAR WILDE (1854–1990), Irish wit and playwright

Reading is to the mind what exercise is to the body.
SIR RICHARD STEELE (1672–1729), founder of the *Tatler*

I can't even spell 'diet'.
GARETH EDWARDS, Welsh rugby union player, while playing in the 1970s

Some days I get up and my knees and hips click, and my shoulders are aching and I wonder if I will still be looking at another eight years at the top.
COLIN JACKSON, British world champion and world record athlete, March 1994

10

Business and Money

Football is business, and business is business.
RINUS MICHELS, Barcelona coach, 1973

HM Customs have now accepted that owning a horse is a business and not a hobby. Accepting advertising (on the horse, etc.) is all part of showing that you are a business concern.
DAVID PIPE, Jockey Club, 1993

Running for money doesn't make you run fast. It makes you run first.
BEN JIPCHO, Kenyan athlete, 1975

If Carl Lewis were to play pro football, he'd have to take a pay cut.
JOE DOUGLAS, Lewis' manager, 1984

The only reason I ever played golf in the first place was so I could afford to hunt and fish.
SAM SNEAD, US golfer

Serguy, I'm just asking you to compete, I don't want to buy the Soviet Union.
ANDY NORMAN, British athletics promoter, to Ukrainian pole vaulter Serguy Bubka, when the latter was seeking $40 000 to appear at Crystal Palace, 1987

He's not going to do it here. He's getting $30 000 to break 20 feet in San Sebastian next week.
ANDY NORMAN to journalists at 1991 World Championships in Seville, after Bubka had won the Gold medal. He did break the record at San Sebastian the following week

Before every competition I am prepared for a record. It depends on many things, but it is not about money.
SERGUY BUBKA, Ukrainian athlete, 1991

I'm going to write a book, *How to Make a Small Fortune in Sport.* You start with a large fortune.
RULY CARPENTER, President of Philadelphia Phillies baseball team, 1976

Baseball has prostituted itself. Pretty soon we'll be starting games at midnight so the people in outer space can watch on prime time TV. We're making a mistake by always going for more money.
RAY KROC (1902–84) of McDonald's, and owner of San Diego Padres, 1976

American football is about many things. Most of all, it's about money.
JAMES LAWTON, sportswriter, *The All American War Game*, 1984

I can make more money out of one hamburger stand than I can out of baseball.
RAY KROC, 1976

When they told me Foreman had beaten Frazier, I thought, my, my, there goes $5 million.
MUHAMMAD ALI, US boxer, 1973

All fighters are prostitutes and all promoters are pimps.
LARRY HOLMES, US boxer, 1984

Sport has to remain sport, a concept rooted in the track and not in the balance sheet.
SEBASTIAN COE, British athlete, in lecture at Yale University, 1982

I would not put my life on the line for a measly million dollars.
LARRY HOLMES, US boxer, before forty-seventh victory against David Bey, 1984

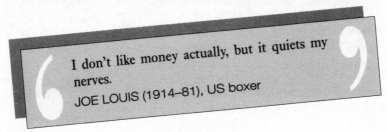

I don't like money actually, but it quiets my nerves.
JOE LOUIS (1914–81), US boxer

I looked upon boxing purely as a business. As a means to an end. Getting the money.
JOHN CONTEH, British boxer, 1981

When you're fighting, you're fighting for one thing – money.
JACK DEMPSEY (1895–1983), US boxer

He is a gangster, he doesn't allow me to stop fighting.
CHRIS EUBANK, British boxer, on the taxman, 1992

Money is the sinews of love, as of war.
GEORGE FARQUHAR (1677–1707), Irish playwright

Money is better than poverty, if only for financial reasons.
WOODY ALLEN, US humorist and film director

Money doesn't talk, it swears.
BOB DYLAN, US songwriter

Money can't buy friends, but you can get a better class of enemy.
SPIKE MILLIGAN, English humorist

When it is a question of money, everybody is of the same religion.
VOLTAIRE (1694–1778), French writer

Come on, we are all harlots – it is all a matter of price. What do you fellows want?
KERRY PACKER, Australian promoter, in cricket negotiations, 1977

Profit isn't a dirty word nowadays. Money is how we keep the score in motor racing nowadays.
COLIN CHAPMAN, racing manager, 1974

When money enters sport, corruption is sure to follow.
E. N. GARDINER, US sportswriter, 1930

An athlete cannot run with money in his pockets. He must run with hope in his heart and dreams in his head.
EMIL ZATOPEK, Czech athlete

If someone is good looking and a medal winner, the combination is almost unbeatable. Then there are those who are very attractive but were also rans. They still have a chance of making money.
NINA BLANCHARD, Head of agency arranging commercial endorsements for athletes after Los Angeles Olympic Games, 1984

When the League offered us 31 matches live, we said, 'Can you deliver?'. The answer was 'Anything can be delivered, so long as the money's right'. I was shattered that they could believe that money is more important than the welfare of the game.
CLIFF MORGAN, former Welsh rugby union player, BBC Head of Outside Broadcasts, 1983

Professional boxing is no longer worthy of civilized society. It's run by self-serving crooks who are called promoters. Professional boxing is utterly immoral. It's not capable of reformation. You'll never clean it up ... mud can never be clean.
HOWARD COSELL, US TV commentator, 1982

Money would probably have made me a dirtier player.
BILL BEAUMONT, English rugby union player and commentator, c. 1990

The money is now so great that it has to stop ... it's obscene. I will never come to terms with the commercial side of the game.
BORIS BECKER, German tennis player, 1991

I believe most sportsmen aren't in it for the money. They start because they love the sport and then the money takes over and they become greedy. Have I got greedy? Oh, yes. But there's not a lot to get greedy about in flat racing.
PETER SCUDAMORE, jockey, 1992

I don't want to be a superstar. I just want to make superstar money.
JAMES WATTANA, Thai snooker player, 1992

It was the most satisfying win of my career and my biggest achievement, but, apart from the winner's cheque for £12 480, I made nothing from it. Not even one endorsement contract.
TONY JACKLIN, English golfer, on winning the 1970 American Open, 1993

What happened to all my dough? I spent it. It cost an absolute fortune to live the life of Riley and I don't regret a single penny.
TONY JACKLIN, 1993

I'm still playing because of the money. If there was no cash around, I'd have gone.
MARTINA NAVRATILOVA, US tennis player, 1991

One of the problems is that 'predominantly white' doesn't sell and we can't keep providing clothes we cannot sell in the shops.
IAN HAMILTON, Nike, on Wimbledon's dress rules, 1992

There are too many 'star' sailors just asking companies to give them £7 million to go off and have fun with the shareholders' money.
CHAY BLYTH, British yachtsman, 1992

I'm very anti-apartheid, but South Africa is a great place to train and the pound goes a long way.
MATTHEW YATES, British athlete, 1992

Blackburn's spending has distorted the finances within soccer. The only hope for the rest of us is for Jack Walker [Blackburn Chairman] to lose interest in football and discover something else, like women.
STEVE COPPELL, football manager, 1993

Motor racing is less of a sport these days than a commercial break doing 150 mph.
PETER DUNN, *Independent on Sunday*, 1992

Whether we like it or not, football and finance go hand in hand.
GEORGE GRAHAM, Arsenal manager, December 1993

Everything's changed now. Money comes before football and money is the ruination.
BILL NICHOLSON, former Spurs manager, December 1993

Tennis is going in the wrong direction and one day it is going to fall apart completely . . . I do not agree with so many tournaments which have a million dollars in prize money and so many computer points. The players between 15 or 20 and 60 make too much money for how good they are and that is a problem, in my opinion. If you have a smaller circuit with fewer big tournaments, a Borg wouldn't stop at 25, nor John McEnroe.
BORIS BECKER, German tennis player, 1991

Every one of our customers without exception are truly grateful to be invited to an event like Wimbledon . . . [it's our way] of thanking them for the business we've received from them.
NAOMI GRAHAM, Hertz, about their corporate hospitality at Wimbledon, 1992

Corporate hospitality is desirable, but not essential. We have to balance it with our prime service to the tennis fans and clubs.
CHRIS GORRINGE, Wimbledon chief executive, 1992

A manager's job is to go out to get the best deal possible for his boxer; the promoter is out for the best deal he can get for himself, keeping the boxer's wages low. A system which allows an individual to be both manager and promoter is wrong; it is the nearest thing to a slave's contract.
BARRY McGUIGAN, Irish boxer, 1990

Brian [Clough] likes a bung.
ALAN SUGAR's evidence in Court concerning alleged illegal payments by his football club, Tottenham Hotspur, 1993

I put together attractions, and then exploit them. First you sign up the attraction, then you make a site deal to host the attraction. You sell it to pay per view and closed circuit ... then you go out and promote the event like it's the second coming . . . that's what I do.
DON KING, boxing promoter, 1993

Sport is a business with a difference. The Board of Management usually do it for nothing, and any surplus is usually reinvested in the sport.
PETER LAWSON, General Secretary of the Central Council of Physical Recreation, 1990

Lemme tell you something. There isn't a person in the world who owns a sports franchise who doesn't own it – to some degree – through his ego. There's something that feeds the ego like nothing else when you own a sports team.
GEORGE STEINBRENNER, owner of New York Yankees baseball club, October 1993

We have a pessimistic point of view of events which are not under our control, such as eleven men kicking a ball about.
MARTIN PROTHERO, Promotions Director for Umbro, suppliers of the England soccer strip, 1993

There would have been no pleasure in winning the Superbowl and still losing money.
JERRY JONES, owner of Dallas Cowboys football team, interviewed in *The Sunday Times*, 8 August 1993

With the £200000 Christie/Lewis affair, have we finally prostituted ourselves to television? I think so. Given the parlous finances of school and club athletics throughout the country, what we'll see chasing the two athletes in Gateshead is a prancing tart, the British Athletic Federation.
DEREK JOHNSON, Management Board, British Athletic Federation, complaining about the Christie/Lewis head to head 100 metres, 1993

I would never dream of telling a golfer how to play golf, but professional sport is more than just hitting a golf ball. If a tin of beans comes out of the factory without a label, no one is going to buy it. Marketing is all about putting the label on the tin, so people notice it, recognize it, and buy it.
TERRY COATES, Chairman and Chief Executive of the Women Professional Golfers European Tour, 1993

Money is indeed the most important thing in the world; and all sound and successful personal and national morality should have this fact for its basis.
GEORGE BERNARD SHAW (1856–1950), Irish dramatist, in *The Irrational Knot*, 1905

It cannot be emphasized too strongly that art as such does not 'pay' ... and that the art that has to pay its own way is apt to become vitiated and cheap.
ANTONIN DVORAK (1841–1904), Czech composer, in *Music in America*, 1895

The election of the USA for the 1994 World Cup opened up a gigantic market on every level; players, coaches, administrators, sponsors. ... We increase our revenue and implant our sport in a very promising country where there are already 15 million regular soccer players.
JOAO HAVELANGE, President FIFA, December 1993, in interview with French magazine *L'Equipe*

11

Champions

To be a top sportsman in any field, you need an arrogance; you need to be driven. It can offend people, but you cannot be bothered about that too much. You might regret it later, as I do in a way, but not at the time.
BARRY RICHARDS, South African and Hampshire cricketer, 1991

Some years ago I sparred with Frazier. He whacked me four times in the cobblers, and didn't say sorry once; he was champion so I had to grin and bear it.
JOE BUGNER, British boxer, 1973

Man, I hit him with punches that'd bring down the walls of a city. Lawdy, Lawdy, he's a great champion.
JOE FRAZIER, US boxer, on fighting Muhammad Ali, 1975

It was like death. Closest thing to dyin' that I know of. I was thinking at the end, what am I doin' here, against this beast of a man? But after it's all over, now I want to tell the world that he's one helluva man actually, and God bless him.
MUHAMMAD ALI, US boxer, on fighting Joe Frazier, 1975

One of the many things I like about Stracey as a world champion fighter is that he recognizes and realizes how ruthless his job must be. He wasn't above hitting Lewis low, or after the bell.
FRANK McGHEE, sportswriter, 1976

C'mon you guys, let's try and take this thing seriously.
MUHAMMAD ALI, US boxer, before fighting British boxer Richard Dunn, 1976

When you land a good punch you can feel it in your arm, your shoulder, your hip, your toes, your toenails.
KEN NORTON, US boxer, after knocking out Duane Bobick in round one, 1977

I was so happy I thought I was gonna cry. But I kept things in and I just waved. It wouldn't be right for the world heavyweight champion to be crying.
LARRY HOLMES, US boxer, after beating Ken Norton, 1978

Faldo's got more nerve than me. I couldn't do what he does. Golfers are visible to everyone, their job is harder than mine.
NIGEL MANSELL, motor racing driver, *c.* 1992

To me, he's very boring. He's never in the trees or in the water.
FRED COUPLES, US golfer, on Nick Faldo, 1993

Of the three Yorkshiremen who have scored 100 hundreds, the most beautiful player, by far, was Hutton. The man to play an innings for your life was Sutcliffe. The man to play an innings for his own life was Boycott.
ALAN GIBSON, journalist, 1977

When Nicklaus plays well, he wins, when he plays badly, he comes second. When he plays terrible, he's third.
JOHNNY MILLER, US golfer, 1978

My greatest strength is that I have no weaknesses.
JOHN McENROE, US tennis player, 1978

I would like to reach my potential just one time in my life.
JOHN McENROE, 1984

The fact is that everyone has their time, then you don't have it any more.
JOHN McENROE, 1991

Borg's won Wimbledon four straight times and out there he's just lost an 18–16 tie breaker. You'd think maybe just once he'd let up and say: forget it. But, oh, no way.
JOHN McENROE, 1980

Everyone says that he can't volley, because his ground strokes are so good. He has learned how to volley. It's not textbook, but who cares. It is such hard work playing against him. So many balls come back. It's like taking too many body punches. You are tired by the end.
BRIAN GOTTFRIED, US tennis player, after losing to Bjorn Borg, 1980

In the fourth and fifth sets, I won all the big points, every single one. I don't know how, but at Wimbledon I am always winning these points. It's very strange.
BJORN BORG, Swedish tennis player, 1979

Tennis has to be very careful. Not everyone is a computer. It's very good that we have John McEnroe. I hope we have a couple more.
BORIS BECKER, German tennis player, 1991

The best doubles pairing? John McEnroe and anyone else.
PETER FLEMING, US tennis player, McEnroe's doubles partner for many years, *c*. 1990

The best thing, doesn't matter how little it is, doesn't matter what it is, if you come up with a *plan*, and you have the training, you have to just believe in what you do.
ABDI BILE, Somalian athlete, 1991

I go into every race looking for victory – whether it's a Micky Mouse race or the Olympics.
LIZ McCOLGAN, British athlete, 1993

It is mental power that separates the exceptional from the very good. When they line up for the 100 metre sprint in Barcelona there will be nothing to choose between them, talent for talent, training for training. What separates them is what goes on behind the eyes.
FRANK DICK, British athletics coach, 1992

The first imperative a coach looks for, in a champion, is style – defined as all the movements coordinated to produce the elegance and efficiency appropriate to the particular discipline.
PETER COE, athletics coach, 1992

Meat pies, good beer and plenty of sunshine.
WAYNE CORDY, Australian winner of the USA PGA 1990, on the
Australian formula for producing good golfers

I have a beautiful smile. Three of them. A million dollar smile, a
2 million dollar smile and a 3 million dollar smile. I'm tall, dark and
handsome.
SHAQUILLE O'NEAL, 21, new US basketball 'ultra star', May
1993, on the reasons for his high earnings (playing contract $40
million over seven years, endorsements $35 million).

Only one in two hundred [football apprentices] become real champions,
of world class, and they are readily identifiable at the age of 14 or 15.
BERTIE MEE, former Arsenal manager, on club studies of the
apprentice scheme, 1992

Buying players is more costly than finding them yourself. Youngsters
we can train and mould into the players we want.
TOM BURGESS, (hitting) coach, Kansas City Royals baseball team,
1992

On the day and the time that matters, Coe is the one to watch.
STEVE OVETT, British athlete on fellow-athlete Sebastian Coe,
1986

There is no one secret. It's a matter of signing the best talent available
and working hard with them.
JOE JONES, senior coach, Kansas City Royals, 1992

I never hit a shot even in practice without having a very sharp, in-
focus picture of it in my head. It's like a colour movie. First I 'see' the
ball where I want to finish. Then the scene quickly changes and I 'see'
the ball going there. Then there's a sort of fade-out, and the next
scene shows me making the kind of swing that will turn the previous
images into reality.
JACK NICKLAUS, US golfer, 1992

The hardest thing for any cricketer to work out is what his game is all
about. You have to have a method. Not that you can play the same way
every time, but it is imperative to work out the shots you can and cannot play, and evaluate the pitch and the bowlers and the way to play
them. I used to be much more forceful and dramatic a player, I think,

but now I have grafted on a consistency and conservatism and I am much less flamboyant. I don't destroy the bowling anymore but I believe I have become a better player and more effective for the side.
GRAHAM GOOCH, then England captain, July 1993

It was all a bit of a fluke really. I didn't know at the time what I was starting. Some people thought it was significant but I don't think anyone really grasped what was happening. I certainly didn't. But kids saw something that was different and fun and they all wanted to try it.
DICK FOSBURY, US athlete, August 1993, twenty-five years after a leap and style that changed the face of world high jumping.

British heavyweights are like buses – you wait a hundred years and then three come along at once.
JOHNNY NELSON, Britain's third heavyweight champion (WBF version), December 1993

Tell all the world, if Sonny Liston whups me I'll crawl across the ring on my hands and knees, kiss his feet, tell him he's the greatest, and leave the country. He's too ugly to be champ . . . he's so ugly that when he cries the tears run down the back of his head . . . I saw

Sonny Liston shadow box the other day and the shadow won . . . set the traps Ah'm goin' bear hunting . . . I'm the real champ. Look at me, I'm beautiful. I am the Greatest.

I don't want to be just heavyweight champion of the world. I'm gonna be champion of the whole universe. After I whup Sonny Liston, I'm gonna whup those little green men from Jupiter and Mars. And lookin' at them won't scare me none because they can't be no uglier than Sonny Liston.
CASSIUS CLAY (later Muhammad Ali), US boxer, part of his daily 'conversation' with the media before the world title fight with Liston, 1964

> Float like a butterfly, sting like a bee.
> Tell Sonny I'm here, I'm ready to rumble.
> Round eight to prove I'm great.
> Bring that ugly bear here now . . .
> CLAY at the weigh-in v. Liston,
> 25 February 1964

I knew I had him in the first round. Almighty God was with me. I am the greatest. I shook up the world. Look at me, I don't have a mark on my face. I'm the prettiest and I'm the greatest. . . . I shook up the world . . . I'm the prettiest thing that ever lived. I am the greatest.
CLAY after Liston failed to come out for the seventh round, 1964

I'm still the champ. I'm still the prettiest. I'm still the greatest. That old Sonny, I wish I could tell him I was only jiving. Didn't mean half of it. Sonny Liston was the greatest – till I came along.
MUHAMMAD ALI, US boxer, on a visit to Scotland, 1993

Sometimes when I visit him on his farm at Michigan, I get the feeling his life force is spent. It's as though he's had enough of his life. I guess being Muhammad Ali for fifty years kinda wears you out.
JIMMY ELLIS, Ali's former sparring partner, also a former heavyweight boxing champion, January 1994

12

Coaches and Coaching

Class in a football coach is, when they finally run you out of town, to look like you're leading the parade.
BEP GUIDOLIN, sacked Tennessee manager, 1976

A man can seldom – very, very seldom – fight a winning fight against his training; the odds are too heavy.
MARK TWAIN (1835–1910), US writer and wit

The players make the coach. The coach who thinks his coaching ability is more than the talent he has is an idiot.
JOE LAPCHICK (1900–70), US basketball player and coach

I don't have nightmares about my team. You gotta sleep before you have nightmares.
BEP GUIDOLIN, coach to American football team Kansas City Scouts, 1975

The coach's job is 20 per cent technical and training and 80 per cent inspirational. He may know all there is to know about tactics, technique and training, but if he cannot win the confidence and comradeship of his pupils he will never be a good coach.
FRANZ STANFL, Austrian athletics coach, 1955

Coaching is to inform, educate and encourage.
GORDON JAGO, English football manager, 1974

Italy's second goal was the ultimate answer to Revie's dossiers: 'Watch Causio, he is apt to leap 2 ft in the air as he receives a pass, sell a dummy while doing so, flick the ball past a defender with an instep and disappear with a puff of smoke'.
DAVID LACEY, sportswriter, *Guardian*, 1976

If Seb doesn't win gold it will be defeat for him but failure for me.
PETER COE, athletics coach, Moscow, 1980 (about his son Sebastian)

For a footballer, it's like living in a box. Someone takes you out of the box to train and play ... and makes all your decisions. I have seen players, famous internationals, in an airport lounge all get up and follow one bloke to the loo. Six of them maybe, all standing there and not wanting a piss themselves, but following the bloke who does. Like sheep.
GEOFF HURST, English footballer, 1977

Consistency, training regularly – you've got to have goals, you've got to have very high ambition, but within that framework of ambition, consistency of training is the single most important thing.
JOHN LANDY, Australian athlete, c. 1987

Consistency, without any doubt at all, is the key element. It's not how many miles you do a week, it isn't how many training sessions you can cram into a three week period if you are going to be injured for another three weeks. It is planning the training so that it is consistent work. And not consistent over one season or one winter, but consistent over 10, 12, 15 or 20 years. Because in athletics nothing good happens overnight.
SEBASTIAN COE, British athlete, 1990

In Japan ... our coach taught that 24 hours is training – even sleeping, eating – we are eating for training, we are sleeping for training. Not sleeping for sleeping. For good training we need food, for good training we sleep and for good training we take a rest.
SHINETSU MURAO, Japanese marathon runner and coach, 1993

I found in my career that I wanted to race, because I knew I had done more training than anyone else, and better training than anyone else, and I wanted to test that in a race.

Confidence comes from preparation more than winning ... confidence is a fragile thing that can be broken fairly quickly, but not if it's from preparation.
RON CLARKE, Australian athlete, 1992

An athlete has to prepare himself physically and mentally. Mental is the key thing for any athlete – that he's determined, that he can win in any event.
KIP KEINO, Kenya athlete, *c.* 1987

Self-confidence isn't just about winning and losing. It's about your work with perhaps a coach, or the attitude of your family towards what you are doing, if you are getting support.
SEBASTIAN COE, British athlete, 1987

The perfect result is 0–0. Goals are scored by defensive mistakes.
ANNIBALE FROSSI, Italian international footballer and coach

If there is any difficulty in the matter of coaching, I would strongly recommend schoolmasters to get in touch with the Amateur Athletic Association with a view to asking the governing body to send out some expert old champion to give the boys a few hints.
FREDERICH WEBSTER, *Athletics of Today*, 1925

The idea of coaching is not to change people, but to talk to them, to prod them, to elicit reactions. No two bowlers in the world of cricket have ever been the same, so there's no one way to do it. What you have to try and do is to maximise individual ability.
JOHN SNOW, England fast bowler, *c.* 1990

I want him to walk on water and not scare the fish.
BILL BYRNE, University of Oregon athletic director, on qualities
needed in a basketball coach, 1992

Coaches are best when people barely know they exist. Not so good
when people obey or acclaim them. Worse when they despise them –
fail to know people – they fail to honour you. But of good coaches
who talk little – when their work is done, their aim fulfilled, their
charges will say – 'we did this ourselves'.
Adapted from LAO-TZU, *Tao Te Ching*, sixth century BC

Coaching a national side is a tremendous commitment, a job in itself.
You have to find the hours from somewhere, something has to go to fit
it all in, and that's usually the family life. There is no short cut to
preparing the side. To be fair to the players you have to do all the
preparation ahead of the training sessions.
IAN McGEECHAN on announcing retirement as Scotland's rugby
union coach, January 1993

Robert Frost said something about the poet's craft: 'The individuality
of the words is at least as important as their union'. Can you see how
that relates to coaching? That had a profound effect on me.
DAVE SEXTON, English football manager, 1993

Have a go, you mug. That means, don't die wondering whether you
were good enough to win; don't wait until you've lost to see if you can
win.
BOB DWYER, Australian rugby union coach, 1991

Players who look to the bench for their solutions should be on the
bench.

The No. 1 in the squash team will never coach or help the No. 2 (the
coach has to do that).

Coaching is an art and a science that promotes creativity. The greatest
accolade is that the people you coached truly believed they did it
themselves.
DAVID WHITAKER, Great Britain hockey coach, 1993

To some the coach is a raging, tracksuited manager of a professional soccer team. To others, it may be a caring middle aged lady who teaches swimming and to yet others the director of a national coaching programme who appears regularly on TV but who may not coach performers at all. We believe that the image of the coach will become clear and positive only when, on the one hand, we have an intelligent, well trained, well deployed and ethically sound coaching force, one which is deeply involved in the major issues affecting their sports, and, on the other, a clear understanding of the roles the coach should play in sport.

Coaching Matters (the review set up by the Sports Council of coaching and coach education in the UK), 1991

There is nothing more difficult to take in hand, more perilous to conduct, more uncertain in its success, than to take the lead in the introduction of a new order of things.

MACHIAVELLI (1469–1527), Italian statesman and writer, *The Prince*, 1513

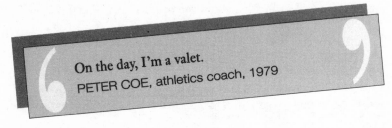

On the day, I'm a valet.
PETER COE, athletics coach, 1979

In Britain you don't have coaches technically capable of taking a kid to world ranking. ... In Germany, I ask a kid like Boris Becker to jump and he asks, how high? In Britain, they ask why?

ION TIRIAC, tennis coach, 1992

The reality is that you are on your own. The German Federation invested more in Becker than the Lawn Tennis Association spent on the coaching programme for the southeast of England.

ANDREW DAVIES, British Davis Cup player, 1991

The first thing I have to teach them is that they can win. We have to open their eyes, give belief.

OLGA MOROZOVA, Russian tennis coach, on her appointment to coach British girls, 1990

There are certain ways the body works the best and you learn to take that material and incorporate it into teaching athletes.
TOM TELLEZ, coach to Carl Lewis, 1993

A coach is like a winemaker: he must produce the best wine with the grapes available.
FABIO CAPELLO, AC Milan's coach, speaking after the departure of Dutch stars Gullit and Rijkaard, 1993

PT exercises, skipping, throwing a medicine ball about, and the endless, endless business of running around the pitch.
DANNY BLANCHFLOWER (1926–93), Tottenham Hotspur and Northern Ireland footballer, on training methods during his early days in football, when balls were rarely used, in *The Double and Before*, 1961

If God had wanted football to be played in the air, he wouldn't have put grass on the ground.
BRIAN CLOUGH, football manager

One of the great problems with sport in this country is that we prefer to play games rather than practise the skills of them. To aim for sporting perfection is seen as taking things too seriously.
DICK BEST, England rugby union coach, December 1993

It is the jigsaw principle. Every single piece has to be in place. One lost piece and there is no finished jigsaw. It is as simple as that.
MALCOLM ARNOLD, Wales national athletics coach, and coach to world champion Colin Jackson, on getting promising athletes to the top, March 1994

You have to like them as people. And if I feel they haven't the talent to start off with, then I'm not really going to be interested.
BETTY CALLAWAY, coach to Torvill & Dean, about choosing dance couples to work with, February 1994

If I don't practise for one day, I know it; if I don't practise for two days, the critics know it; if I don't practise for three days, the audience knows it.
IGNACE JAN PADEREWSKI (1860–1941), Polish pianist, composer and patriot

13

Commentators
(Serious)

You are the best sports commentator I've ever heard: exact, enthusiastic, prejudiced, amazingly visual, authoritative and friendly. A great pleasure to listen to you.
DYLAN THOMAS (1914–53), Welsh poet, writing to John Arlott, June 1947

I talk about what I see. A lot of commentators tend to talk about what they are thinking rather than what they are watching.
JOHN ARLOTT (1914–91), English cricket commentator

Not since he wished viewers a Happy New Year has Frank Bough ever quite said precisely what he means.
DENNIS POTTER (1935–94), English playwright, 1978

I don't make mistakes. I make prophecies which are immediately proved wrong.
MURRAY WALKER, British motor racing commentator

Vocabulary – that's my biggest failing. I try very hard to think of something clever or witty to say when a ball goes into the net but I usually end up saying, 'Oh, what a goal!'
JOHN MOTSON, British football commentator

Americans believe Dan Maskell invented television; he invented tennis and Wimbledon.
BUD COLLINS, US tennis commentator, 1992

It's the same sort of technique whether you're talking about a skier coming down a mountain or a bit of 36-24-38 walking down a platform.
DAVID VINE, British snooker and skiing commentator

14

Commentators
(Less Serious)

The par here at Sunningdale is 70 and anything under that will mean a score in the sixties.
STEVE RIDER

Stuart Pearce has got the taste of Wembley in his nostrils.
JOHN MOTSON

Hodge scored for Forest after only 22 seconds, totally against the run of play.
PETER LORENZO

Sadly, the immortal Jackie Milburn died recently.
CLIFF MORGAN

And now for the goals from Carrow Road, where the game ended 0–0.
ELTON WELSBY

And Keegan was there like a surgeon's knife . . . bang.
BRYON BUTLER

With the very last kick of the game, Bobby McDonald scored with a header.
ALAN PARRY

He went down like a sack of potatoes, and then made a meal of it.
TREVOR BROOKING

And umpire Dicky Bird is gestating wildly as usual.
TONY LEWIS

I'm glad to say that this is the first Saturday in four weeks that sport will be weather free.
DAVID COLEMAN

The whole crowd is rising to its feet to applaud this man Bryant who is perhaps, without doubt, arguably, the greatest bowler of all time.
ALAN WEEKS

And that's the third time this session he's missed his waistcoat pocket with the chalk.
TED LOWE

Watch the time – it gives you a good indication of how fast they are running.
RON PICKERING

For those of you with black and white sets, Liverpool are in the all–red strip.
DAVID COLEMAN

And Wilkins sends an inch perfect pass to no one in particular.
BRYON BUTLER

We don't always get from slow motion the pace at which they play.
JOHN BARRETT

Born in Italy, most of his fights have been in his native New York.
DESMOND LYNAM

It's a unique occasion really – a repeat of Melbourne 1977.
JIM LAKER

I'm not one to blame anyone, but it was definitely Viv Richards' fault.
FRED TRUEMAN

A fairy dream came true.
BILL BEAUMONT

They've got old shoulders on their heads.
J. P. R. WILLIAMS

And Shaun Edwards has happy memories of Wembley; on his last appearance here he received a fractured cheekbone.
RAY FRENCH

You can cut the tension with a cricket stump.
MURRAY WALKER

Are there any more great swimmers in the pipeline?
CLIFF MORGAN

There's going to be a real ding dong when the bell goes.
DAVID COLEMAN

Azinger is wearing an all black outfit: black jumper, blue trousers, white shirt and a pink tea cosy hat.
RENTON LAIDLAW

Roscoe Tanner is one of the great runners-up of all time. No man could have played better.
DAN MASKELL

I never predict anything and I never will do.
PAUL GASCOIGNE

So over to the ringside – Harry Commentator is your carpenter.
BBC announcer

Never go for a 50–50 ball unless you are 80–20 sure.
IAN DARK

BRIAN MOORE: 'Ray Houghton was clearly 4 or 5 yards offside'.

RON ATKINSON: 'Yes, but for me that's when Houghton is at his most dangerous'.

Tony Meo is eyeing up a plant.
DAVID VINE

The batsman's Holding, the bowler's Willey.
DON MOSEY, BBC cricket commentator (who said he had been waiting a long time for this opportunity).

The wife of the Oxford President is kissing the cox of the Oxford crew.
Unidentified BBC boat race commentary

Let's give a big Johannesburg welcome to the West Indies.
WANDERERS' public address greeting to the visiting Pakistan cricket team, February 1993

MIKE CHANNON: 'We've got to get bodies in the box. The French do it, the Brazilians do it, the Italians do it . . .'

BRIAN CLOUGH: 'Even educated bees do it.'
Exchange on ITV, 1986

Welcome to Bologna on Capital Gold for England against San Marino with Tennant's Pilsner Lager brewed with Czechoslovakian yeast for that extra Pilsner taste and England are one down.
JONATHAN PIERCE's radio commentary for England's last World Cup qualifying match v. San Marino, in Bologna, November 1993

He's the race of voicing.
RICHARD PITMAN on his BBC commentator colleague Peter O'Sullivan

Ray Illingworth has just relieved himself at the Pavilion end.

Neil Harvey, standing at leg slip with his legs wide apart, waiting for a tickle . . .
BRIAN JOHNSTON (1912–1994), English cricket commentator

15

Contracts

First thing we do, let's kill all the lawyers.
Dick the Butcher in SHAKESPEARE, *Henry VI, Part ii*, 1594

Nastase's new contract is 35 pages long and 15 of them are devoted to penalties about his behaviour.
JERRY BUSS, manager of Los Angeles Strings, 1977

When I left Yorkshire I received a letter from the Secretary saying they were not going to offer me a contract which began 'Dear Ray Ellingworth...' But they had crossed the 'Ray' out. They couldn't even bring themselves to call me by my first name or use a fresh piece of paper.
RAY ILLINGWORTH, English cricketer, 1978

International athletes these days don't need a coach. They need a lawyer.
STEVE CRAM, British athlete, August 1987

I'm last in line at Williams and it's humiliating. The world champion is last in line. What a story ...! Some drivers grow the fruit, others come in and pick it.
NIGEL MANSELL, motor racing driver, 1992

The secret of life is honesty and fair dealing. If you can fake that you have got it made.
GROUCHO MARX (1895–1977), US humorist

It's just as unpleasant to get more than you bargain for as to get less.
GEORGE BERNARD SHAW (1856–1950), Irish dramatist, in
Getting Married, 1908

I don't think contracts mean anything to Eric. If he wants to walk out he probably will do.
MARTIN EDWARDS, Manchester United Chief Executive, on Eric
Cantona, December 1993

16

Courage and Fear

Keep your fears to yourself, but share your courage with others.
ROBERT LOUIS STEVENSON (1850–94), Scottish author

There is blood on my typewriter, blood on my notes, blood on my programme. And however long I live I will never forget the face of Ron Stander standing up to Joe Frazier. The face of courage in tears.
PETER WILSON, sportswriter, 1972

What helped me develop my quickness was fear. I think the rougher the opponent, the quicker I am.
US boxer SUGAR RAY LEONARD before second fight with Roberto Duran, 1980

There is no such thing as bravery; only degrees of fear.
JOHN WAINWRIGHT (born 1921), British author

I'm a hard man. I can look at you hard enough to make tears come out of your eyes. And I'm a proud man, I do whatever I got to do. . . . I hit Ali punches, those punches, they'd have knocked a building down. And he took 'em.
US boxer JOE FRAZIER on Muhammad Ali, the 'Thriller in Manila'

Of course, I'm scared, I'm always scared. But you just overcome fear, harness it. At the end it's all energy.
CHRIS EUBANK, British boxer, January 1993

I'm sort of a calm person. I'm not incredibly brave. I'm only as brave as my horse. Some riders are much braver than that; they will take a chance ride and gallop around a cross country course. Not me.
MARY THOMSON, British equestrienne, May 1993

Human beings inspire more fear in me than Arctic expeditions.
SIR RANULPH FIENNES, British explorer, July 1991

Courage is almost a contradiction in terms. It means a strong desire to live taking the form of a readiness to die.
G. K. CHESTERTON (1874–1936), English critic, novelist and poet

Some people are born with a certain sense of excitement. Some people like things that are a little more conservative, other people like to push the limit a little bit – I have always been one of those people who would like to walk that final line.
ANDY MILL, US skier, 1992

You don't think about fear, or how dangerous it's going to be because you know you have trained for it. I know what I am able to do and I know I can do it. That's in a time difference of hundredths of a second, and you can't explain how you thought about it, how to handle it, it is just you feel it and you do the right thing.
PETER WIRNSBERGER, downhill skier, 1992

Downhill skiing is the classic fight or fright syndrome. The only thing I want to do when I am going fast is – go faster. You don't think. There is no thought process in skiing. You react like an animal.
STEVE PODKORSKI, joint world champion, 1982

I am in greater danger each time I drive my own car than in a Formula One race. On the track, I have no cars coming towards me, and I am with experienced, professional drivers. And we all know our cars and their limits.
STEFANO MODENA, Tyrrell racing driver, 1992

It was very difficult to drive afterwards, but that was our profession.
JUAN FANGIO, Argentinian motor racing driver, speaking in 1992 of the death of a team-mate in the German Grand Prix in 1954

It's the only thing I know how to do. The thought of getting back into motor racing is the only thing that keeps me going. It beats working for a living.
MARTIN DONNELLY, English motor racing driver, who suffered multiple injuries after crashing at 170 mph at Jerez in Spain in 1990

It is all down to the fine tuning; the fine tuning of my car, its chassis and balance, and my body, my heart and my brain. To be at my peak I need to have them all together at their peaks at the right time. For me it is a task and a challenge every time I drive.
AYRTON SENNA (1960–94), Brazilian motor racing driver, 1992

The coward is not a man and to fight bulls men are necessary.
PEDRO ROMERO (1754–1839), Spanish matador, reputed to have killed 5600 bulls between 1771 and 1779

I know very well what they want, and one of these days I might just give it to them to keep the bastards happy.
MANOLETE (1917–47), Spanish matador, 1946

The aficionados go for one reason; to see the almost death of the matador.
JOSEPH CONRAD (1857–1924), English novelist

I don't fear nothing if I'm in good shape, even when they shout, 'Benn, it's your time'. But if I think I haven't prepared myself right, then I'm in the wrong frame of mind. Otherwise the ring don't hold no fear for me. Why be in the game if you're scared?
NIGEL BENN, British boxer, 1993

People go because there is an element of danger. They go to see knock-outs, to see men hurt. That's why the heavyweights are the most popular.
COLIN HART, boxing writer, 1992

To say that I climb 'because it is there', is a bit fatuous, but through risking your life you come alive. By going to the limits of endurance you come back a changed, altered person, more awake and renewed – you are able to deal better and more objectively with the ups and downs of ordinary life.

Sometimes it's almost as if it's written that a climber would die on a particular expedition. It does not make me want to give up mountaineering or climbing.
DOUG SCOTT, mountaineer, 1992

You just have to treat death like any other part of life.
TOM SNEVA, US racing driver, 1977

On the day of a big motor race, a lot of people want you to sign something just before you get into the car, just so they can say they got your last autograph.
A. J. FOYT, US motor racing driver, Indianapolis 500, 1976

Only twice in my career was I afraid: once in a club game against Neath, and then against Canterbury.
GARETH EDWARDS, Welsh rugby union player, reflecting on the infamous match v. Canterbury on the British Lions tour of New Zealand in 1971

Tennis players have more or less been put on a stage. I think we need to be even closer to the people who watch us. You can't live with fear.
STEFFI GRAF, German tennis player, after incident with a man who slashed his wrists in front of her, 1989

I'm not afraid to die. I just don't want to be there when it happens.
WOODY ALLEN, US humorist and film director

That secret of heroism, never to let your life be shaped by fear of its end.
GEORGE BERNARD SHAW (1856–1950), Irish dramatist, 1898

I suppose in a perfect world boxing wouldn't belong, but millions of people want to see it. And you've got to ask, whose life is it anyway?
Boxing promoter MICKY DUFF, May 1992

I hung it out there much too much today. The track is full of fast bends and I was going into them so quickly. I did not know whether I had the grip or not to come out the other side. All the time, you are doing it, there is a tremendous fight going on inside you. One part is saying 'try it', but another is saying 'be careful'. You are exceeding all the limits you know, driving on the absolute maximum. I did it today but I hope I don't do it tomorrow. In the circumstances we are competing in, I do not think it is worth the effort of pushing yourself beyond the limit. It is a great feeling when it comes off, but if you get it wrong, you realize you are risking your life – the risk element is too high. But today my heart was speaking higher than my reason.
AYRTON SENNA (1960–94), Brazilian motor racing driver, at Spanish Grand Prix, May 1993

17

Determination – The Will to Win

I can lick my weight in wildflowers.
W. C. FIELDS (1879–1946), US humorist

I'm throwing twice as hard as ever I did. The ball's just not getting there as fast.
'LEFTY' GOMEZ (1908–89), New York Yankees' baseball pitcher

If you see a tennis player who looks as if he is working very hard, then that means he isn't very good.
HELEN WILLS MOODY, US tennis player

Let's get our retaliation in first.
CARWYN JAMES, British Lions rugby union coach, New Zealand, 1971

Morale is when your hands and feet keep on working when your head says it can't be done.
ADMIRAL BEN MOREELL (1892–1978), US navy commander

Come on. No, wait! Get back. . . . Sorry!
GEOFFREY BOYCOTT, English cricketer

Some time ago I asked Ian Botham whether he had always been an aggressive sportsman. He shamelessly revealed that he often used to get sent off when he was playing Under 11s football at school.
MIKE BREARLEY, English cricketer, 1979

I have always had a tremendous desire to be top scorer in the League or whatever competition or whatever game. If I have scored two in the first half and don't get one in the second I will be disappointed.
GARY LINEKER, English footballer, 1991

This club's history is based on and steeped in passion. The vast majority of my players tonight played as if they had never been told that passion is what Liverpool is all about.
GRAEME SOUNESS, Liverpool FC manager, after losing to Bolton Wanderers in the FA Cup, January 1993

He has a Stalinist attitude. It wasn't enough to beat somebody; you had to destroy them, defeat their system, their reasoning, their belief.
British athlete SEBASTIAN COE on fellow-athlete Daley Thompson, 1992

What I need most is somebody to make me do what I can.
RALPH WALDO EMERSON (1803–82), US poet/essayist/philosopher

Even Mozart had to put in the hours.
PROFESSOR JOHN SLOBODA, arguing that most people could become accomplished musicians, 1993

I've got a woman's ability to stick to a job and get on with it when everyone else walks off and leaves it.
MARGARET THATCHER, Secretary of State for Education, February 1973

I've always been self-confident – very conscious of what I am and what I can and cannot do. For the past few years people have been telling me to be patient and that my time would come. Sod it. My time is now, not in the future.
VICTOR UBOGO, English rugby union player, December 1993

I will keep on trying until I do the swim. It will be a hell of a thing to finish – as good as the Olympics. I am hooked on it.
Olympic gold medallist ADRIAN MOORHOUSE on his attempt to swim the English Channel, August 1993

Miracles have to be worked for with honesty and effort. I am a realist where truth and work are concerned.
GLENN HODDLE, Chelsea FC manager, August 1993

If you watch a game, it's fun. If you play at it, it's recreation. If you work at it, it's golf.
BOB HOPE, US entertainer and amateur golfer

There are a lot of rewards but there's also a lot of sacrifice. I don't drink, I watch what I eat and I don't have any social life. When you get up at 7.30 in the morning and do a 17 mile run, there's no way you can go out in the evening.
LIZ McCOLGAN, British athlete, world 10 000 metre champion, 1992

If at first you don't succeed, try again. Then give up. No use being a damn fool about it.
W. C. FIELDS (1879–1946), US humorist

18

Drugs

Reality is just a crutch for people who can't cope with drugs.
LILY TOMLIN, US actress

Cocaine is God's way of saying you're making too much money.
ROBIN WILLIAMS, US comedian and actor

Drugs have taught an entire generation of American kids the metric system.
P. J. O'ROURKE (born 1947), US humorist, *American Manners*, 1983

Avoid all needle drugs – the only dope worth shooting is Richard Nixon.
ABBIE HOFFMAN, US radical activist, *Steal This Book*, 1971

Now they're calling drugs an epidemic – that's 'cos white folks are doing it.
RICHARD PRYOR, US comedian and actor, in *Richard Pryor Here and Now*, 1984

My grandfather couldn't prescribe a pill to make a greyhound run faster but he could produce one to make the other five go slower.
BENNY GREEN, British journalist, 1972

I'm so full of dope that if you stood around me with a headache, it'd go away.
Irish golfer DAVID FEHERTY, recovering from a snake bite, 1992

If you were looking for indications in recent years of performance enhancement, I would not think that Welsh rugby was the natural starting point.
DENNIS EVANS, Secretary of Welsh rugby union, 1991

In the old days of competition, people would cluster around the champions asking them about their exercise routines. Now they just ask – what drugs are you on?
ROGER WALTER, bodybuilder, third in Mr Britain, 1973

There are only two alternatives to taking anabolic steroids – don't take them and be second class, or give up athletics.
HOWARD PAYNE, British athlete, 1974

Much of the drug-taking in athletics would stop if other athletes were not having to keep up with the American Joneses.
SIR ARTHUR GOLD, President of European Athletics Association, 1985

Cocaine arrived in my life with my first round draft in the NFL. It has dominated my life. . . . Eventually, it took control and almost killed me. Cocaine may be found in quantity throughout the NFL. It's pushed on players. . . . Sometimes, it's pushed by players. Just as it controlled me, it now controls and corrupts the game, because so many players are on it.
DON REESE, American footballer, in *Sports Illustrated*, 1982

I've yet to meet an Olympic or world class weight lifter who hasn't felt that taking steroids has been beneficial to his performance. Athletes would like not to take steroids. They don't feel right or good about it, but they're afraid not to, because they're concerned about what the next athlete might be doing.
DR IRVING DARDIK, Chairman of US Olympic Sports Medicine Commission

While the vast majority of athletes would no more take drugs than jump off Beachy Head, there are cheats at the margins and they have to be weeded out.
SEBASTIAN COE, British athlete, 1989

I knew it couldn't be detected, because the IOC's lab equipment hadn't been programmed to identify furazobol.

It was clear that steroids were worth approximately a metre at the highest levels of sport.
CHARLEY FRANCIS, Canadian coach to Ben Johnson, 1989

> I can tell you that Ben Johnson is very much against drugs. He has never taken them and he never will.
> CHARLEY FRANCIS, Canadian athletics coach, and coach to Ben Johnson, 1987

[Getting the news] was the ultimate horror . . . like a fatal car crash: you knew it could happen at any time but you never believed it could happen to you.
CHARLEY FRANCIS, *Speed Trap*, 1990

Ben Johnson used steroids and got two years. I used Alka Seltzer Plus and may get life.
LARRY MYRICKS, US athlete, after failing test, 1991

One of my dreams is to run as well as Ben Johnson did . . . but I intend to do it cleanly.
JASON LIVINGSTONE, British athlete, shortly before failing a drugs test, 1992

Jason Livingstone wasn't doing it in isolation. There's at least three or four people who knew what he was doing.
DALEY THOMPSON, British athlete, 1992

You have to be suspicious when you line up against girls with moustaches.
MAREE HOLLAND, Australian athlete, 1988

They dare not. It is as simple as that. Because many of them are absolutely terrified that more than one or two of their precious superstars would be shown to be drug users and as guilty as hell.
PETER CONI, British sports administrator, on why all governing bodies do not introduce effective drug testing procedures, 1993

75 per cent of our work has to do with drug abuse. I used to count medals, now I count urine samples.
HELMUT MEYER, announcing he would not seek re-election as President of German track federation, 1992

I am not like other athletes that have been busted for anabolic steroids. I have evidence that I didn't do it. Other athletes break down in the end and admit it. Not me. I have nothing in my closet to hide and I have *evidence*.
BUTCH REYNOLDS, US athlete, 1993

It is this Court's conclusion that the IAAF's hearing was not conducted in good faith, was not conducted by an unbiased decision maker, was not in accordance with the IAAF's own rules and regulations, did not accord Reynolds a full and fair opportunity to participate and resulted in a decision that was not fair and impartial but rather was arbitrary and capricious. ... The evidence before the Court establishes that the IAAF's goal throughout these proceedings was – and remains – solely to protect its reputation and that of the LaFarge Laboratory.
Written judgement, US District Court, Southern District of Ohio, Eastern Division (awarding Reynolds $27.3 million in lost earnings and punitive damages).

It is not Butch against the IAAF, it is athletes against the IAAF.

Neither the IAAF nor any man can confuse me or take away my focus. I did two and a half years for no reason. I was a prisoner. Now I want a gold medal.
BUTCH REYNOLDS, 1993

One national track star's diet: Vitamin A, 1600 mg; B-complex capsules, four times a day; vitamin C, 200 mg; vitamin B6, 150 mg; calcium tablets, four daily; magnesium tablets, twice a day; zinc tablets, three per day; royal jelly capsules; garlic tablets; cayenne tablets; eight aminos; Gamma-Oryzanol; Mega Vit Pack; supercharge herbs; Dibencozide; glandular tissue complex; natural steroid complex; Inosine; Orchic testicle extract; Pyridium; Ampicillin; and hair rejuvenation formula with Biotin.
And that was what he ADMITTED to taking!
ROBERT VOY, former chief officer to the US Olympic Committee, in *Drugs, Sport and Politics*, 1991

The information that they received was that the drug testing for the first time in history was to be so accurate as to diagnose the use of anabolic steroids and other drugs. . . . Certain athletes chose to leave – rather than be tested. A lot of athletes didn't trust drug testing; it was something new . . . they didn't want to be subject to something they weren't sure they could trust.
ROBERT VOY on the withdrawal of American athletes from the 1983 Pan American Games in Caracas, when 21 medal winners were still tested positive and disqualified, 1991

Someone is told on 11 December that on 11 January a policeman will be waiting at the end of his driveway to inspect his driver's licence . . . only a fool would not have things in order when he runs into the policeman.
ROBERT VOY, on drug testing procedures, 1991

People want to win, and drugs are a short cut. Once you're an Olympic champion your life is totally different. Opportunities come that you would not otherwise have had. And 1980s society is full of greed and getting ahead. It's just win at all costs.

But I couldn't go to an athlete and say you need drugs because, for me, that would be telling them I don't believe in you.
PAT CONNOLLY, US athletics coach, 1992

We used anabolic steroids strictly according to medical considerations. The state of wellbeing of the athlete was meticulously analysed and . . . checked. . . . According to my knowledge no country in the world has treated its athletes better, even after the end of their careers.

The starting point was the Montreal Olympics. We knew what the Americans were doing – and we wanted to stay in competition.
DR MANFRED HOPPNER, director of the competitive sport
section, East German Medical Sports Association, 1990

We encourage young people to take up sport because it is good for them, physically and mentally; we think it is good for character development. The last thing we should do is bring them into something with the potential danger that drugs carry.
SEBASTIAN COE, British athlete, 1992

If sport was really cleaned up effectively, the number of national records being set would drop drastically and that ... sells sport around the world. ... The public pay to see events, see athletics; they want to see bigger than life; they want to see records broken.
DR CHARLES YESALIS, Penn State University, on the sports
administrators' problems with drugs, 1992

After working hard for so many years and then watching the Eastern European athletes up close, we suspected they were using drugs, although not knowing them as kids we couldn't see the changes; but we could sort of dismiss it and say, well, we're better than they are. But, when the American women started using drugs we could see them change. We could hear their voices deepen, we could see the beard appear on their faces and their muscle definition completely change. We could see them going from mediocre, weak athletes to these incredibly powerful, gifted super athletes, and I'm talking about women.
PAT CONNOLLY, US athletics coach, 1992

How many men have you ever met who weighed 280 lbs, who have a fairly narrow waist, and who are as quick as the devil and can run as fast as can be? I don't believe I've ever met anyone like that. But you'll see a whole lot of them every time you watch an NFL football game.
DR ROBERT KERR, American adviser to several Olympic athletes,
1992

I am convinced that the problem is widespread not only in Canada but also around the world. The evidence shows that banned ... substances and in particular anabolic steroids are being used by athletes in almost every sport, most extensively in weightlifting and in track and field.

Despite knowing the fallacy of in-competition testing, as they have for many years, [the IAAF] have taken no steps to make the fallacy more widely known.
CHIEF JUSTICE CHARLES DUBIN, head of the official Canadian Inquiry into drug abuse in sport, 1988

We lost our innocence as a sporting nation in Seoul.

Many of these organizations (national and international) have been not much more than indifferent to the fight against drugs in sport. . . . It is unfortunate that the IAAF has not used its influence in a more meaningful way to eradicate the drug problem . . . (its) posture appears to have been to react to the problem only after the fact.

The last sixteen years of in-competition testing has been largely a waste of time and money.

[There is a] decline in ethical values which pervade modern day sporting competition.
ROBERT ARMSTRONG, QC, Chief Counsel to the Dubin Inquiry, 1988

As a society we have been very unwilling, or maybe unable, to deal with our addiction to sports and winning.
STEVE COURSON, US footballer, 1992

When I'm competing in a game and the only difference was the other guy was beating me because he was taking drugs then I have two choices – I stop or I take drugs as well.
BORIS BECKER, German tennis player, 1990

Only the foolish and the ill-advised get caught.
SIR ARTHUR GOLD, Chairman of the British Olympic Association, and leading anti-drug campaigner, 1990

We could find a thimbleful of a banned substance in a swimming pool.
PARK JONG SEI, test director at Seoul Olympic Games, 1988

There are many, many more substances for which it is impossible to test.
PROFESSOR ARNE LJUNGQVIST, Chairman of IAAF Medical Commission, 1988

I can take testosterone today and pass the test tomorrow. No officials are addressing the issue of women and drugs.
PAT CONNOLLY, US athletics coach, 1992

They've all turned a blind eye. Their feeling is, if we haven't caught any, we haven't got any. Why? Because it means more TV, more money, more trips for the boys.
DALEY THOMPSON, British athlete, 1992

A little bit of the joy went out of the sport for me today. I think it's tragic ... something was terribly wrong. The distances were always pure and not tainted. Now I feel it's a tainted mark.
LYNN JENNINGS, Olympic 10 000 metre bronze medallist, commenting after Wang Junxia of China lowered the world record for the distance by 42 seconds (in the next week, Chinese runners also broke the 1500 and 3000 metre records), 1993

I believe these girls are taking drugs. You just can't go out and run those times, certainly not at 20. You can't take these records seriously.
JOAN ALLISON, former British athletics team manager, on the Chinese women runners' achievements, 1993

I would not blame Liz if she decided to chuck it. What's the sense of running against the Chinese? She may as well run against men.
PETER McCOLGAN, husband of former 10 000 metre world champion, Liz, 1993

Well, she's certainly not eating porridge.
INGRID KRISTIANSEN, former 10 000 metre world record holder, on China's Wang Junxia, after suggestion that she was training on a diet including caterpillar fungus and boiled turtle, 1993

Some people in the West say, 'Oh, these people are using drugs', but in fact it is them who are using drugs. I have never seen any drugs. I do not even know what drugs are.

The turtles are very nutritious, the blood and oil is good.
MA JUNREN, Chinese athletics coach, 1993

Better to lose twice than to cheat once.
FRANZISKA VAN ALMSICK, fifteen-year-old gold medallist at European swimming championships, 1993

It's not enough to catch a stable lad with a smoking syringe.
ROGER BUFFHAM, head of security at Jockey Club, on problems of gaining doping convictions in racing, 1993

He won't be the last. When I went to the South American champion-ship in 1977, from a squad of 30 players, 20 were on drugs. Some were addicts and some were occasional users.
CARLOS BILARDO, Seville coach and former Argentina manager, on footballer Claudio Caniggia's positive test for cocaine, 1993

I said after the Seoul Olympics that I would come back and compete clean. I know that I did.
BEN JOHNSON, announcing his enforced retirement, 1993

This is a clear cut test of testosterone doping. I can see no reasons or grounds that the results can be contested.
PROFESSOR ARNE LJUNGQVIST, Chairman of IAAF Medical Commission, confirming Johnson's positive drug test, 1993

Politics has taken over from principles. ... Despite the known serious deficiences in testing, IAAF officials pontificate that the record-breaking Chinese athletes cannot be using doping agents because their tests yield negative results. Similar statements were made about East German authorities for many years during the time they were scientifically and ruthlessly doping their athletes by using known gaping holes in dope control procedures. ... They 'catch' athletes for minor offences or by doubtful practices to indicate productivity rather than face the fact that the system has now become fatally flawed.

PROFESSOR ARNOLD BECKETT (past member, International Olympic Committee Medical Commission), in letter to *The Times*, London, 6 January 1994

Razors pain you
Rivers are damp;
Acids stain you;
And drugs cause cramp.
Guns aren't lawful;
Nooses give;
Gas smells awful;
You might as well live.

DOROTHY PARKER (1893–1967), US writer and wit, in *Enough Rope*, 1926

Cocaine isn't habit forming. I should know – I've been using it for years.

TALLULAH BANKHEAD (1903–68), US actress

19

Excellence and Experience

The triumph of hope over experience.
DR SAMUEL JOHNSON (1709–84), English lexicographer, referring
to the hasty remarriage of an acquaintance following the death of
his first wife, with whom he had been unhappy (from Boswell's *Life
of Johnson*), 1791

Few things are harder to put up with than the annoyance of a good
example.
MARK TWAIN (1835–1910), US writer and wit

The best is the enemy of the good.
VOLTAIRE (1694–1778), French writer

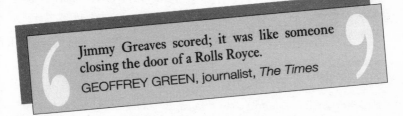

Jimmy Greaves scored; it was like someone
closing the door of a Rolls Royce.
GEOFFREY GREEN, journalist, *The Times*

We learn from experience that men never learn anything from
experience.
GEORGE BERNARD SHAW (1856–1950), Irish dramatist

Experience is a comb that Nature gives to men when they are bald.
Eastern proverb

Experience is not what happens to a man. It is what a man does with what happens to him.
ALDOUS HUXLEY (1894–1963), English novelist

Our blend of youth and experience worked well. The experienced players stood around watching youngsters do all the work.
GRAHAM GOOCH, English cricketer, after victory over Pakistan in Texaco Trophy, 1992

So often does Lewis use the words 'focus' that the press occasionally run a book on how many times he will use it within the space of one news conferencee. It is a word not misused by him, for his focus for more than twelve years has been phenomenal.
DAVID MILLER, journalist, on US athlete Carl Lewis, *The Times*, 1993

One of those men who reach such an acute limited excellence at twenty-one that everything afterward savours of anti-climax.
F. SCOTT FITZGERALD (1896–1940), US novelist, *The Great Gatsby*, 1925

If men could learn from history, what lessons it might teach us! But passion and party blind our eyes and the light which experience gives is a lantern on the stern, which shines only on the waves behind us!
SAMUEL TAYLOR COLERIDGE (1772–1834), English poet, *Biographia Literaria*, 1817

His divots go further than my drives.
DAVID FEHERTY, Irish golfer, on US golfer John Daly, 1993

I thought, Christ, you don't get that in the ZDS Cup.
TIM FLOWERS, England goalkeeper, after first cap against Brazil, reporting to the media that England manager Graham Taylor had warned him that the Brazilians might shoot from corners, 1993

The problem is that when you get it [experience], you're too damned old to do anything about it.
JIMMY CONNORS, US tennis player, 1988

Fair Play and Gamesmanship

The tradition of baseball always has been agreeably free of chivalry. The rule is, 'Do anything you can get away with'.
HEYWOOD BROUN (1888–1939), US journalist and novelist

A gentleman is one who never strikes a woman without provocation.
H. L. MENCKEN (1880–1956), US journalist

Serious sport has nothing to do with fair play. It is bound up with hatred, jealousy, boastfulness, disregard of all rules and sadistic pleasure in witnessing violence; in other words it is war minus the shooting.
GEORGE ORWELL (1903–50), English novelist, from *The Sporting Spirit*, 1945

It's good sportsmanship to not pick up lost golf balls while they are still rolling.
MARK TWAIN (1835–1910), US writer and wit

Headmaster: 'Of course, my standards are out of date. .... standards are always out of date. That is what makes them standards.'
ALAN BENNETT, English writer and wit, *Forty Years On*, 1968

When a man has pity on all living creatures, then only is he noble.
BUDDHA (*c.* 563–483 BC), founder of Buddhism

Show me a good loser in professional sport and I'll show you an idiot. Show me a good sportsman and I'll show you a player I'm looking to trade.
LEO DUROCHER, US baseball manager

No man can think clearly when his fists are clenched.
GEORGE JEAN NATHAN (1882–1958), American critic

He could not see a belt without hitting below it.
MARGOT ASQUITH (1865–1945), on her Prime Minister husband's
great rival Lloyd George

Quit fouling like a wimp. If you're gonna foul, knock the crap outa
him.
NORM STEWART, Missouri Tigers basketball coach, to 6 ft 9 in.
Dan Bingenheimer, 1992

Let's see how stiff that upper lip is when it's split.
JEFF THOMSON, Australian cricketer

No leadership, no ideas. Not even enough imagination to thump
someone in the line-out when the ref wasn't looking.
J. P. R. WILLIAMS, Welsh rugby union player after Wales' defeat
by Australia, 1984

For nothing can seem foul to those that win.
Henry IV in SHAKESPEARE, *Henry IV, Part ii*, 1600

Every team has a clogger whose job it is to put a clever opponent out
of the match.
HARRY CATTERICK, football manager, 1971

Football managers don't look on county cricketers as professionals,
but just because they enjoy themselves they are no less professional.
There is more comradeship in cricket and nowhere near so much
backstabbing as in football. Cricketers always accept defeat, footballers cannot.
JIM CUMBES, Aston Villa footballer, Worcestershire cricketer,
c. 1985

Anyone who engages in competitive sport accepts that there must be
rules and referees and umpires to enforce them. If the rule book is
torn up or vicious fouls go unpunished, then the sporting element is
destroyed and the fun for both the player and the spectator is lost.
SIR MICHAEL HAVERS, British Attorney General, 1978

In sport, in courage, and in the sight of Heaven, all men meet on equal terms.
Prime Minister SIR WINSTON CHURCHILL (1874–1965)

In football, it is widely acknowledged that if both sides agree to cheat, cheating is fair.
C. B. FRY (1872–1956), English footballer, cricketer and athlete, 1911

If you spend a lot of time on sportsmanship, you're going to spend a lot of time losing.
GLEN DOBBS, Tulsa coach

Spitting is part and parcel of the game now.
GEORGE GRAHAM, Arsenal manager, defending Ian Wright, 1991

He who hates vices hates mankind.
THRASEA (died AD 66), Roman philosopher

If you're up against a girl with big boobs, bring her up to the net and make her hit backhand volleys.
BILLIE JEAN KING, US tennis player, *c.* 1980

Croquet seems to appeal particularly to Wall Street types: unlike golf you're manipulating your opponent rather than the ball.
JACK OSBORN, US Croquet Association

Gamesmanship, if it's in the mind, is beautiful in the sense that you can use your mind and body in conjunction. You're using them in the same way as you can imagine chess – your body is the piece and your mind is the player.
STEVE OVETT, English athlete, *c.* 1990

For when the great scorer comes to write against your name,
He marks, not how you won or lost, but how you played the game.
GRANTLAND RICE (1880–1954), American sportswriter

The complaint of Pakistani cheating is a wild accusation and a reflection of [England's] colonial hangover. They should learn to accept defeat graciously instead of calling others a cheat.
IMRAN KHAN, Pakistani cricketer, 1992

I didn't have a clue what was going on. I thought perhaps Imran had something stuck in his boot.
ALLAN GREEN, Sussex cricketer, on being asked to take a bottle top out to his captain Imran Khan for ball adjustments, 1981

Pakistan's entire match strategy is based upon getting the ball to reverse swing at some point during the match. Every Pakistan team member knows exactly how this is achieved and begins working towards that moment – usually after 35–40 overs – when Wasim and Waqar begin to find late movement. The methods which achieve this are against the rules.
DEREK PRINGLE, English cricketer and journalist, November 1993

Rugby football is a game for gentlemen in all classes, but never for a bad sportsman in any class.
Motto of Barbarians Rugby Football Club

Cricket is a hot blooded game. We mustn't be too critical if young men, stretched to the limit, boil over.
TED DEXTER, Chairman of the Cricket Selection Committee, 1993

Roy was just too clean cut. He staked his reputation on qualities like courage and honesty – things which just aren't so fashionable to talk about any more.
Roy of the Rovers Editor, DAVE HUNT, on the demise of the comic hero, 1993

I decided that if I was going to compete with the best I had to be as aggressive and get the psychological edge on my opponent without going over the top.
WADE DOOLEY, English rugby union player, 1993

England have swapped 'fair play' and 'it's only a game' for the cold-hearted ruthlessness which is a far better reflection of the Anglo-Saxon soul than the twee virtues shaped by the Victorian forebears of rugby union.
EDDIE BUTLER, former Wales rugby union captain, journalist, 1993

Promoter Don Stuart put on a clean show and demonstrated that boxing need not be brutal or crooked.
Plaque (State History Marker No. 243) outside what is now the Sheriff's office, Carson City, Nevada, commemorating Corbett v. Fitzsimmons world heavyweight title fight, March 1897

I think you'd have got that, don't you?
JACK NICKLAUS to Tony Jacklin, respective Ryder Cup captains, saving Jacklin a difficult, short putt and thus halving the USA v. Britain match, 1969

Say it ain't so, Joe.
A group of small boys encountering Chicago White Sox hero, 'Shoeless Joe' Jackson, outside stadium, after revelations that the White Sox 'threw' the baseball world series, 1919

There is no room for cheats in the sport. Cheating only brings failure in the end, and you get caught out, everyone gets caught. There is still room in athletics for those who are honest and work hard to succeed at the top.
JOHN WALKER, New Zealand 1500 metre gold medallist, c. 1992

Foul play and cheating are the two factors that can make the game unplayable . . . the All Blacks are guilty of both . . . international rugby players are among the most physical yet literate and I believe they know exactly what they are doing.
CLEM THOMAS, Welsh rugby union player and writer, December 1993

The All Blacks will be remembered mostly as a dirty side. That is sad for them. But I think they deserve it. The Phil de Glanville and Kyran Bracken incidents, plus several more, went beyond the unwritten code among players.
WILL CARLING, England rugby union captain, after All Black tour Autumn 1993, in which England defeated New Zealand at Twickenham

For evil to triumph, all that is needed is for good men to do nothing.
EDMUND BURKE (1729–97), Irish statesman and philosopher

We have to protect the schemers, the thinkers. For years, players have been cutting them down by all means. Those players call themselves artists but, in any other cultural activity, I don't know where a competitor deliberately tries to injure an opponent. We have no alternative but to instruct the referees to apply the laws very strictly.
SEPP BLATTER, FIFA General Secretary, December 1993

It's a bit of a joke those guys querying my not walking. I played here for eight years and I know Australians don't walk.
KEPLER WESSELS, South African Test captain, after criticism by Allan Border (as captain of Queensland) for not walking after a 'catch' at the wicket, December 1993

Remember, men, we're fighting for this woman's honour; which is probably more than she ever did.
GROUCHO MARX (1895–1977), US humorist, *Duck Soup*, 1933

The 'doped' conker has arrived. People cut them in half and fill them with Polyfilla.
JEFF CLOVES, author of the *Official Conker Book*, on changes to the rules in the World Conker Championships, 1993

Playful talk about playing to the referee has become more blatant talk of cheating. The word is becoming commonplace.
GERALD DAVIES, former Wales and British Lions rugby union player, journalist, 1993

21

Fame

Being a celebrity is like being raped. You can't do anything about it.
JOHN McENROE, US tennis player, 1985

Fame is something which must be won; honour is something which must not be lost.
ARTHUR SCHOPENHAUER (1788–1860), German philosopher

I hate the big time. I feel the loss of close friends. I have to have bouncers at my birthday parties now.
JAMES HUNT (1947–93), English motor racing driver, 1976

If I get a £5 speeding fine, it's all over the front pages. If I win the Grand Prix of Rotterdam, one of the greatest of all titles, the back pages don't even mention it.
HARVEY SMITH, British showjumper, 1974

I mean, fame's quite fun and all that, but as soon as anything goes wrong or you make a big bog of something, everyone knows about it, and that does taint it a bit.
LUCINDA PRIOR-PALMER (now Green), British equestrienne, 1976

I guess I'm not the same anymore ... I feel sort of different since I got my picture in the newspapers. ... Like I'll be driving and some guy will cut me off, you know, and I'll think to myself, just who is this guy, cutting me off? When did he ever get his picture in the papers? It's like I know I'm not a nobody anymore.
JOHN McENROE, US tennis player, 1977

Racing can't afford to lose jockeys like Steve [Cauthen]. Like top class footballers and cricketers, he puts spectators through the turnstiles. On a rainy night at Redcar or Leicester, he would put 10 per cent on the gate.
Owner ROBERT SANGSTER after news of Cauthen's retirement, 1993

If I had to do it all again, I wouldn't, it's not worth it. If I had a choice, I would just be a normal person.
ZOLA BUDD-PIETERSE, South African athlete, 1992

I lost all my growing-up years. I haven't lived a normal life, I think it was a mistake.
SEVERIANO BALLESTEROS, Spanish golfer, on taking up pro golf too early, 1992

Mikhail Gorbachev will always be known as the man who placed Russia, the Soviet countries and Eastern Europe on the map of professional boxing.
JOSE SULAIMAN, President of the World Boxing Council, 1991

Getting caught in a scandal is my biggest fear. I've spent a life building something positive and I know any mistake could damage that for the rest of my life. People look to their role models to be almost flawless. ... It's hard to live up to something like that, really harder than basketball. It's really the biggest job I have.
MICHAEL JORDAN, US basketball player, 1992

Arnie has more people watching him park the car than we do out on the course.
US golfer LEE TREVINO on Arnold Palmer, May 1993

Everyone wondered about Suzanne [Lenglen], what she would look like. Everything is too simple in tennis now. Wouldn't it be neat to be a mystery woman and bring high fashion to the sport? To be like Suzanne, like Madonna – out there but untouchable? Like, unreachable?
MONICA SELES, US tennis player, 1993

The first response to my win was that it was good that a British woman could go out, do it clean and succeed. Many had doubted that it was possible. But I have had this feeling since of jealousy – an impression that some begrudge me making it because it proves that anybody can if they do the work.
SALLY GUNNELL, British Olympic gold medallist, September 1993

Everyone wants a piece of you and it is difficult getting used to that. More than anything, you begin to value time on your own.
SALLY GUNNELL, December 1993

Men, women, boys and girls cheered him to all his centuries, running his runs with him. The gods had been good to him – and he was good to us.
NEVILLE CARDUS (1889–1975), English music critic and cricket writer, on Denis Compton, 1947

I was in the lobby of the hotel talking to [Seve Ballesteros] and the receptionist came over and asked me, 'Are you Mr Ballesteros?' and I said, 'No, he is', of course, but the next day I go out and shoot 67 because someone thinks I'm Seve Ballesteros.
Irish golfer DAVID FEHERTY, at the Volvo German Open, 1993

People say they wish they were Michael Jordan. OK, do it for a year. Do it for two years. Do it for five years. When you get past the fun bit, then go do the part where you get into cities at 3 a.m. and you have 15 people waiting for autographs when you are as tired as hell.
MICHAEL JORDAN, US basketball player, June 1993

Ian Botham is being sued for not visiting enough pubs. No jury will ever believe that.
Sun leader, 28 July 1993

I never said, 'I want to be alone'. I only said, 'I want to be LEFT alone'. There is all the difference.
GRETA GARBO (1905–90), Swedish actress

Fame is sometimes like unto a kind of mushroom, which Pliny recounts to be the greatest miracle in nature, because growing and having no root.
THOMAS FULLER (1608–61), English historian, *The Holy State and the Profane State*, 1642

Fame is the spur that the clear spirit doth raise
(That last infirmity of noble mind)
To scorn delights, and live laborious days.
JOHN MILTON (1608–74), English poet, *Lycidas*, 1637

Love of fame is the last thing even learned men can bear to be parted from.
TACITUS (*c*. AD 55–120), Roman historian, *Agricola*, *c*. AD 98

He's comfortable in his celebrity. He has a flair, is colourful, has multi-interests and is a giving person. And he's come at the right time.
PAT WILLIAMS, general manager of Orlando Magic basketball team, on Shaquille O'Neal, December 1993

Over Christmas, I think I had my picture in the newspapers more than John Major. It's always the same.
VINNY JONES, Wimbledon FC, December 1993

I don't know if I enjoy being in the limelight, but being England centre forward it's inevitable. I get recognized in the street – and not just where I live.
KAREN WALKER, Doncaster Belles football team, 1993

A celebrity is a person who works hard all his life to become well known, then wears dark glasses to avoid being recognized.
FRED ALLEN (1894–1956), US humorist

22

Famous Last Words

Some people are on the pitch. They think it's all over . . . it is now!
KENNETH WOLSTENHOLME, commentating on the World Cup
soccer final, Wembley, 1966

So many beautiful girls. I couldn't take my eyes off them. And they
kept touching my hair. Swedish people had not seen many blacks at
that time.
PELE, Brazilian footballer, reflecting in 1992 on his first World Cup
in Sweden in 1958

Terry will look after the 11 players on the field. I will look after the
£11 million at the bank.
Businessman ALAN SUGAR, when first taking over Spurs with
Terry Venables, 1991

Everything I have done in life has prepared me for this job.
TED DEXTER on appointment as Chairman of the Cricket Selection
Committee, 1989

NOW will you believe me.
The hypochondriac's epitaph

The days of women's cricket being seen as a knicker parade must be
over.
NORMA IZARD, manager of England's World Cup winning team,
1993

We're not looking for a minor miracle, we're looking for a major one.
GRAHAM TAYLOR, England football manager, before San Marino
World Cup match, November 1993

Canadian weightlifters; Three clean and four jerks.
Graffiti in Canada after four of their weightlifters were caught on
drug offences at Seoul Olympic Games; October 1988

There is a silence where hath been no sound
There is a silence where no sound may be,
In the cold grave –
Under the deep, deep sea.
THOMAS HOOD (1799–1845), English poet

I have a dream that the brotherhood of man will become a reality. With this faith I will go out and carve a tunnel of hope from a mountain of despair.
MARTIN LUTHER KING (1929–68), US clergyman and civil-rights leader, his last address 24 hours before his murder

Kids imitate champions. If they try to imitate Fosbury he will wipe out an entire generation of high jumpers because they will all have broken necks.
PAYTON JORDAN, US coach, in Mexico 1968, as Dick Fosbury won the gold medal with a new Olympic record of 7 ft 4.5 in and established a new style of jumping

I had to take two extra valium because I thought the dress was going to lose.
TEDDY TENLING, tennis dress designer, July 1978 having designed a 'lucky' dress for Martina Navratilova

McEnroe is the last player to win with beauty instead of brute force.
MANUEL SANTANA, Spanish tennis player and commentator, July 1989

Hopefully people will remember the way I played the game rather than the way I acted at times.
JOHN McENROE, US tennis player, 1990

I had pro offers from the Detroit Lions and Green Bay Packers, who were pretty hard up for linemen in those days. If I had gone into professional football the name Jerry Ford might have been a household word these days.
GERALD FORD, US President, February 1974

23

Fans

C'mon the whites!
Bored cricket watcher, 1978

Alcoholism v. Communism.
Banner at Scotland v. USSR, soccer World Cup, 1982

Someone has to pay for Cinderella's ticket to the ball, and as usual it's
the poor old fan.
Visiting fan from Oxford commenting on paying £14 at the
reconstituted Valley ground of Charlton Athletic Football Club, 1993

They think they are the ultimate judge of what is going to happen,
and think they have the right to boo. And if you want my opinion,
they are right.
LUCIANO PAVAROTTI on being booed by the audience at La
Scala after missing a note in Don Carlos, 1993

Abroad the crowd is too far from the players. Here the game is
warmer. There is even room for love between the crowd and players.
The crowd vibrates with the game.
ERIC CANTONA, Manchester United footballer, December 1993

It was guilt that I felt. Because you're so close to it and that you're
thinking you should be with them, but you're not, you are still alive.
Hillsborough disaster survivor in report by National Institute for
Social Work, 1993

You go to other people's grounds, you run 'em, it's just enjoyment all
the time. Like a tennis player gets all geared up to play, we get geared
up to fight. . . . Tribal, innit? Football is one tribe onto another. . . .
We fight because we like fighting. If they banned drink we'd still fight.
English football fan, quoted in *Hooligans Abroad*, Williams, Dunning
and Murphy, 1984

Violence at domestic football matches is sporadic and local and associated with a comparatively small number of clubs . . . its prevention depends upon the effective application of measures locally. . . . We understand the concern to seek an absolute, even a draconian, solution to this problem, but we believe that none exists which is both reliable in its effect and fair in its impact.
Report of Government Working Group, *Football Spectator Violence*, 1984

This move has been forced on us and is a very sad testimony to the state of the world we live in.
TED CROKER, FA General Secretary, on the Government ordered transfer of the annual England v. Scotland match from London to Glasgow, 1985

I am ashamed of the ground and I am ashamed when people come to Bradford and look at the ground. In a nutshell, it is a shit pit.
STANLEY HIGGINBOTTOM, Chairman of Bradford City Football Club, after fire in which over 50 lost their lives, 1985

Liverpool fans have brought shame and disgrace to their country and to football.
Prime Minister MARGARET THATCHER, after Heysel Stadium disaster, 1985

If this is what football has become, let it die.
L'Equipe, on Heysel disaster, 1985

My God, why are these vandals allowed to leave the island? Never again let these visitors into a stadium.
Bild Zeitung, 1985

Soccer has been swamped, as though by a foul poison, by a persistent strain of criminal violence that grew out of the game's peripheral problems, but has now utterly abandoned the host that gave it its original life. . . . For the cure to its crisis, football has to look further than its own disciplines and rules. The game is no longer the thing. The game has gone.
The Times leader, 1985

Peace, peace is what I seek and public calm;
Endless extinction of unhappy hates.
MATTHEW ARNOLD (1822–88). Words repeated in Mr Justice Popplewell's report on football violence, to the British Government, 1985

This is major adventure – one of the few authentic adventures left for young working-class men, to travel away for a few days to a foreign place they know nothing about. There's always a risk that something might go off.

It's exciting. It's away from the banalities of everyday routine and existence, away from the domestic constraints which normally tie you down. It's a real opportunity to give free rein to a very narrow and chauvinistic sense of what being English is about and the best place to display it is abroad.
JOHN WILLIAMS, Senior Researcher, Norman Chester Centre for Football Research at Leicester University, October 1993

Football hooligans? Well there are 92 club Chairmen for a start.
BRIAN CLOUGH, football manager, 1980

No one likes us, we don't care.
Fans' chant at Millwall FC, at friendly v. Sporting Lisbon to open new stadium, 4 August 1993

A game for hooligans run by hooligans.
DAVID EVANS, MP, former Chairman of Luton Town FC, 1993

There is no known cure.
Prime Minister JOHN MAJOR, on being a Chelsea fan, 1993

Get off my pitch!
BRIAN CLOUGH, football manager, to supporter running on the
Nottingham Forest pitch, before striking him; Clough later
apologized and was fined £5000 by the FA, 1992

The first televised case of the shit hitting the fan.
Press comment on the incident.

**People object to being beaten by volunteers rather than the Police. We
told the volunteers that if they wanted to beat somebody they should
take them outside and do it. We are taking this matter very seriously.**
G. Y. LELE, Joint Secretary of the Indian Cricket Board of Control,
on the behaviour of spectators, 1993

**When I got the ball, even before I did anything wrong, I was getting
booed. But it's part and parcel of football.**
JOHN BARNES, after England World Cup match v. San Marino,
1993

**After all the expectancy, the tickets on the mantelpiece for weeks, the
pre-match pints, the bouncing optimistic trek through achingly
English 'Just William' villas ... what a letdown. When will we ever
learn? And yet, as the sun sank slowly behind the old West Stand,
nostalgia and memories took a grip and the jovial, jolly banter rose
and fell on the haunting aroma of mulled red wine. One sensed that
soon all would be forgotten and forgiven. The rugby's only incidental, after all. ...**
COLIN WELLAND, English writer (including *Chariots of Fire*) on
the poor-quality England v. Ireland rugby union international,
February 1994

24

Food and Drink

If the Government banned alcohol, then the Henley Regatta would fold up its tents overnight.
FRANK KEATING, *Guardian*, 1981

I need 6 or 7 pints and half a dozen trips to the gents before I'm ready to play.
ALAN EVANS, Welsh darts player

You can take darts out of the pub match, but you'll never take the pub out of darts.
MART FITZMAURICE, darts referee, 1991

There is no area of nutrition where faddism, misconception and ignorance are more obvious than in athletics.
S. H. and W. R. SHORT, US nutritional scientists, 1983

Baseball players who are usually first into the dining room are usually last in the statistics.
JIMMY CANNON (1910–73), US sportswriter

Everywhere I go in the world, my host offers me only curry.
SUNIL GEVASKAR, Indian cricketer

The most famous recipe in racing is the one for Lester Piggott's breakfast – a cough and a copy of the *Sporting Life*.
SIMON BARNES, journalist, *The Times*, 1992

Recent market research data has shown a high correlation between the profiles of beer drinkers and rugby enthusiasts.
CHRIS ZANETTI, Allied Beer Brands, 1991

We're getting the same food every day. Fortunately, there's a McDonald's here.
JAMES JETT, US Olympic sprinter, in Barcelona, 1992

I've been living on salads, fish and fresh air.
Jockey MICHAEL ROBERTS after dieting to make the weight on
York winner Lyric Fantasy, 1992

I always eat light on fight day.
JAMES J. CORBETT (1866–1933), World heavyweight champion,
after breakfast of 3 chops, two eggs, toast and tea 5 hours before
title fight against Bob Fitzsimmons on 17 March 1897

The doctor told me I should try drinking wine because it would be
good for me. When I did he took one look at me and said, 'You'd better go back on the beer'.
PAUL GASCOIGNE, English footballer, June 1993

Beer is intrinsic to Gascoigne's diet.
CLAUDIO BARTOLINI, Lazio club doctor, 1993

I can't believe Gazza has been pigging out on junk food then making
himself sick.
SALLY ANN VOAK, *Sun* slimming editor, *Guardian*, 3 August 1993

How long have I been off the booze? That's easy: 27 days, 3 hours and
21 minutes.
JIMMY WHITE, snooker player, 1992

I had to choose between tobacco and football and I chose football.
JOHANN CRUYFF, a 40-a-day smoker before his heart operation,
1992

A woman drove me to drink, and I never even had the courtesy to
thank her.
W. C. FIELDS (1879–1946), US humorist

I've squandered fortunes in my life on birds, booze and gambling.
But, as my old pal Stan Bowles liked to say, it's better than wasting it.
FRANK WORTHINGTON, English footballer, August 1993

Pressure never bothered me until I got sober. I've been really stressed
out.
JOHN DALY, US golfer, on life on the dry, 1993

He knew before, and he knows emphatically now, that he can't quit during a round.
DEAN BEMAN, PGA Tour Commissioner, announcing the indefinite suspension of John Daly, 1993

If you drink, don't drive. Don't even putt.
DEAN MARTIN, US entertainer, 1979

And behold joy and gladness, slaying oxen, and killing sheep, eating flesh, and drinking wine:
let us eat and drink; for tomorrow we shall die.
The Bible, Book of Isaiah 22:13

Gatting would have enjoyed this lunch. And that one, and that one over there . . .
GRAHAM GOOCH, English cricketer, speaking at a business lunch, December 1993

I saw a sign saying Drink Canada Dry.
GEORGE BEST, Irish footballer, in cabaret act, asked why he went to America, 1993

I used to quite like turnips but now my wife refuses to serve them.
GRAHAM TAYLOR, England football manager, 1993

For Sport

Sport is the most precious commodity we can hand on to the next generation.
RON PICKERING (1930–91), British athletics coach and BBC commentator

For a small nation sport is very important. Through sport we can advertise ourselves to the world.
MARK TARMAK, Estonian Olympic Committee, 1991

What I find myself doing is reflecting on the rewards of comradeship a simple game gave a lad who was growing up. As boys we were told that sport is about the friends you will make and now I'm an old guy I realize how true that was.
JACKIE KYLE reflecting on 47 caps as Ireland's rugby union fly half, 1992

Through sport boys acquire virtues that no books can give them.
CHARLES KINGSLEY (1819–79), English author

Exercise and temperance can preserve something of our early strength even in old age.
CICERO (106–43 BC), Roman statesman and writer

In sport, in courage, and in the light of Heaven, all men meet on equal terms.
Prime Minister SIR WINSTON CHURCHILL (1874–1965)

Sport is a preserver of health.
HIPPOCRATES (460–377 BC), Greek physician

Sport is our life blood.
Prime Minister JOHN MAJOR, December 1993

> You'll learn as much about life on the basketball court as you will for the rest of your degree.
> BOBBY KNIGHT, basketball coach at Indiana State University, to students, 1992

The sun will shine, the grass will grow and the pitch will be beautiful, I will be able to bowl on it and bat on it, with a bowling machine, to my heart's content.
Prime Minister JOHN MAJOR, choosing a life-sized replica of the Oval as his 'luxury' on *Desert Island Discs*, 1992

Sport is the most unifying influence in the world today.
SIR DENNIS FOLLOWS, Chairman of the British Olympic Association, 1980

Cricket, lovely cricket
(Ramadhin and Valentine
those two little pals of mine)
Calypso lyric, LORD BEGINNER, 1950s

Sport is a wonderfully democratic thing, one of the few honourable battlefields left.
DANNY BLANCHFLOWER (1926–93), Tottenham Hotspur and Northern Ireland footballer, 1982

Sport is a means of providing pleasure to people – it is like offering clothes to those who need them.
ABDUL RAHMAN BUKHATIR, Arabian promoter of the Asia Cup (cricket), 1985

I was in children's homes for nearly 14 years. The Whitbreads adopted me and gave me the security of a family. I felt that through sport I could be on level terms with the world. It was my hobby, my life.
FATIMA WHITBREAD, British athlete, 1993

26

Gambling

There are two times in a man's life when he should not speculate: when he can't afford it, and when he can.
MARK TWAIN (1835–1910), US writer and wit

The way his horses ran could be summed up in a word ... Last.
GROUCHO MARX (1895–1977), US humorist, in *Esquire*, 1972

The sure way of getting nothing for something.
WILSON MIZNER (1876–1933), US playwright

There are two great pleasures in gambling: that of winning and that of losing.
French proverb

Death and dice level all distinctions.
SAMUEL FOOTE (1720–77), English dramatist

There may come a time when the lion and the lamb will lie down together, but I am still betting on the lion.
JOSH BILLINGS (1818–85), US humorist

The race may not go to the swift, nor the battle to the strong, but that's sure the way to bet.
DAMON RUNYON (1884–1946), US author and journalist

£16! How lovely.
HM THE QUEEN on winning Royal sweepstake at Epsom Derby, 1992

I hate football.
Pools winner in a syndicate that picked up £2 million, 1993

They belong to baseball.
Commissioner PETER UEBERROTH restoring to baseball Hall of Fame veterans Mickey Mantle and Willie Mays, banned because of gambling connections, 1985

I have seen thousands of boys and young men, narrow chested, hunched up, miserable specimens, smoking endless cigarettes, many of them betting.
LORD BADEN-POWELL (1857–1941), explaining foundation of Boy Scouts movement, 1907

Even though Lewis is at prohibitive odds, the professional gamblers are going in heavily on him. It's buying money, really. They are looking at it as a better way of earning interest on their money than sticking it in a building society.
GRAHAM SHARPE, the William Hill organization, before the Lennox Lewis–Frank Bruno fight, 1993

If Stan Bowles could pass a betting shop like he can pass a ball, he'd have no worries at all.
ERNIE TAGG, his manager at Crewe Alexandra FC, 1974

Man is a gaming animal. He must always be trying to get the better in something or other.
CHARLES LAMB (1775–1834), English essayist

It's a fair swap. He gets my daughter and I get tickets for rugby internationals.
MIKE CARTER at the wedding of his daughter to England rugby union winger Tony Underwood, 1993

27

Great Sporting Clichés

We're taking each game as it comes.

The manager/boss/gaffer knows what he's doing.

The game's not over till the ref/umpire blows his whistle (till the fat lady sings).

A game of two halves.

End to end stuff.

We got a result.

The selectors have picked what they believe to be the best team/squad/formation for this match/tournament/competition.

This one was/is for the folks at home.

Live and exclusive on . . .

The umpire's made his decision . . . but I was on the front foot . . . well down the track/wicket . . . it was going down the legside . . . it came off the pad . . .

We can only go out there and do our best.

Players win matches; managers and coaches lose them.

You're only as good as your last game.

The horse didn't want it today.

I'm just delighted to be in the squad/team/frame/race/final . . .

William Webb-Ellis: 'Is it a goal, Sir?'
Gamesmaster: 'No, but it was a nice try.'
Rumoured conversation at Rugby School, 1823, after Webb-Ellis picked up the ball and ran thus originating the game of rugby.

The Blazer Brigade.
(Press description of sports administrators)

We wuz robbed

I'm over the moon

I'm sick as a parrot

It just came to me and I stuck it in the back of the net

I was lucky, I guess

I can't believe that referee

We have no comments about the referee

The ball didn't run for us

There's always next year

We did our homework

Let's just say the lads will be in for extra training tomorrow

Cup Final day is a one-off ... current form goes out of the window, and it's on the day. I'm a great believer – if your name's on the Cup you will definitely win it ... we'll first have to wait and see ...
Former football manager TOMMY DOCHERTY when asked who he thought would win the FA Cup, 1994

... AND SO ON ...

28

Health, Fitness and Medicine

I know I'm really fit when my workmates tell me how ill I look.
STEVE CRAM, British athlete, 1988

Athletes live a life quite contrary to the precepts of hygiene, and I regard their mode of living as a regime more favourable to illness than to health.

While athletes are exercising their profession, their body remains in a dangerous condition, but when they give up their profession, they fall into a condition more parlous still; as a fact, some die shortly afterwards; others live for some little time but do not arrive at old age.
GALEN (*c*. AD 130–201), Greek physician

The whole imposing edifice of modern medicine is like the celebrated Tower of Pisa – slightly off balance.
HRH PRINCE CHARLES

Our own history, perhaps better than the history of any other great country, vividly demonstrates the truth of the belief that physical vigour and health are essential accompaniments to the qualities of intellect and spirit on which a nation is built.
President JOHN F. KENNEDY (1917–63), 1962

After a match, if Italian footballers go out for a meal, they sit down. They don't stand around on tired legs. They look upon their bodies as machines and they don't fill those machines with alcohol.
GRAEME SOUNESS, Scottish footballer and manager of Rangers FC, 1991

Sport is a preserver of health.
HIPPOCRATES (460–377 BC), Greek physician

There's only one winner in professional boxing. I have never known a promoter suffering from punch drunkenness or brain damage.
JAMES CALLAGHAN, MP, 1991

I swear my sons will never pick up a cue. Snooker can seriously damage your health.
ALEX HIGGINS, the 'People's Champion' Irish snooker player

Gosh, how times have changed. When I was playing rugby, it was a dangerous game, but sex was safe.
DR TONY BROWNE, Irish RFU President, on AIDS, 1992

You could see the fear on people's faces. Did he bandage it? Is it alright? Is it leaking? You know, that whole thing.

There's one big job I've got left now: that is to change people's attitudes. I got to do better there. If they feel this way about me, they feel this way about everybody.
'MAGIC' JOHNSON on his second retirement from basketball to campaign on AIDS; after cutting his arm at an exhibition match in Charlotte, USA, 1993

This idea that runners do not require washing after violent exercise no doubt arose from the abhorrence of trainers of the old school of cold water. The usual method was for the trainer to take the chill off the water by filling his mouth and blowing it over his charge's back. With the help of a rough towel this produced a fine polish upon the skin, which was held to be a sure sign of fitness.
HAROLD GRAHAM, *Athletics of Today*, 1901

Professional sport has nothing to do with health.
YULY KRELIN, Russian surgeon, *c.* 1990

If they're so bleedin' fit, why are they so bleedin' tired at the end of the season?
GEORGE BEST, Irish footballer, on the modern player, at the House of Commons, 1993

Paul [Gascoigne] is only 50 per cent fit after his crazy summer.
DR BARTOLINI, Lazio doctor, 1993

Our shot putters are in better condition than Gazza.
LINFORD CHRISTIE, British athlete, 1993

It seems to me a typical triumph of modern medicine to find the only part of Randolph that is not malignant and remove it.
EVELYN WAUGH (1903–66), English novelist, on hearing that Randolph Churchill had a non-malignant tumour removed from his lung.

Young ladies should take care of themselves. Young ladies are delicate plants. They should take care of their health and their complexion. My dear, did you change your stockings?
JANE AUSTEN (1775–1817), English novelist, *Emma*, 1816

Only do always in health what you have often promised to do when you are sick.
SIGISMUND (1368–1437), Holy Roman Emperor, advice on achieving happiness

There are three things you lose as you get older. Your memory, and then, er, and then ...
GUNNAR ERICSSON, 74, Swedish member of the International Olympic Committee, 1993

Heroes and Heroines

There used to be a time when the idea of heroes was important. People grew up sharing myths and legends and ideals. Now they grow up sharing McDonalds and Disneyland.
BOB DYLAN, US songwriter, 1992

One day, Ben Johnson was Superman: the human bullet, the fastest in the world. The next day, he was a drug taking, cheating black man; the human pin cushion. And the world queued up to condemn him, as they are doing now to Tyson.
SIMON BARNES, journalist, *The Times*, 1992

We need never fear an objective analysis of our heroes. Truth is ultimately more enlightening and satisfying than myth.
THOMAS REEVES, *A Question of Character*, 1991

The son sees the awesome power of Doc Gooden and thinks there has never been a power pitcher like him; the father sees Doc Gooden and thinks of Bob Gibson; and the grandfather sees the same player and thinks of Bob Feller.
DAVID HALBERSTAM, *Baseball: The Perfect Game*, 1992

Youngsters need heroes. They need figures like Batman, Tarzan and Naas Botha.
ABIE MALAN, South African rugby manager, 1992

It's a sad trait of being English that we shoot down our sporting heroes as soon as anything goes wrong. The past is forgotten.
ALEC STEWART, England cricketer, on his captain Graham Gooch, May 1993

Brilliant. Tell him he's Pele.
JOHN LAMBIE, Partick Thistle manager, on being told that his striker Colin McGlashan had a head injury and temporarily did not know who he was, 1993

30

Hype

Once every five or ten years there comes the fight of the century.
DAN DUVA, boxing promoter, on Evander Holyfield v. Mike Tyson,
1991

It is a champagne sponsorship that will bring a bubble, sparkle and
zest to our Cup.
GORDON McKEAG, Football League President, on Coca Cola's
sponsorship of the League Cup, 1992

People are always kicking, old or young. Even an unborn child is
kicking.
SEPP BLATTER, FIFA General Secretary, on football's worldwide
appeal, 1992

Keegan is Newcastle through and through. The fire is burning and
we're not going to put it out.
FREDDIE FLETCHER, chief executive Newcastle United, December
1993

'Agincourt, Waterloo, Twickenham.
Nike adverts before England v. France rugby
union international, January 1993'

31

Individuals and Individuality

In Heaven an angel is nobody in particular.
GEORGE BERNARD SHAW (1856–1950), Irish dramatist

We are merely the stars' tennis balls,
struck and bandied
which way please them.
JOHN WEBSTER (1580–1625), English dramatist, in *The Duchess of Malfi*, 1623

For my part, I run with a clear goal before me; I am like a boxer who does not beat the air; I bruise my own body and make it know its master, for fear that after preaching to others I should find myself rejected.
The Bible, 1 Corinthians 9:26–7 (quoted about British athlete Gordon Pirie, by H. Hicks, at his Memorial Service, February 1992)

Resistance to the organised mass can be effected only by the man who is as well organised in his individuality as the mass itself.
CARL JUNG (1875–1961), Swiss psychiatrist

There's no style left in cricket, no individuality. Players should wear numbers on their backs now so you can tell them apart.
TREVOR HOWARD, British actor, 1974

'Christ, why do you wear that hat?'
'Because nobody likes it.'
Reply by CHRIS LEWIS on his first England tour to West Indies 1989/90

Why runners make lousy Communists.

In a word, individuality.

It's the one characteristic all runners, as different as they are, seem to share . . .

Stick with it. Push yourself. Keep running.

And you'll never lose that wonderful sense of individuality you now enjoy.

Right, Comrade?

Nike advert for running shoes at 1984 Olympic Games in Los Angeles

Now they'll surely learn to spell and say my name right.

Welsh golfer IAN WOOSNAM, about the US media, after winning the Masters title, 1991

He says what he feels and his language at times leaves you thinking, oh, my God. That's Gascoigne. The downside helps to make these people what they are – the Gascoignes and the Bothams.

GARY LINEKER, English footballer, 1992

I don't know if circumstances will change. Maybe it will be here I find stability. Maybe not. It is not something I'm looking for. Maybe I'll want it when I'm older. The main thing is to live for pleasure.
ERIC CANTONA, French footballer, on life at Manchester United, January 1993

Eric will always be in my team, but I have the impression that, if he can't score a beautiful goal, he'd rather not score. I'd like him to score an ugly one now and again.
MICHEL PLATINI, French footballer and manager, on Cantona, 1992

There is a modern fashion for designer stubble and some people believe it to be very attractive. But it is aggravating to others and we will be looking at the whole question of people's facial hair.
TED DEXTER, Chairman of the Cricket Selection Committee, 1993

No one said anything about designer stubble when Graham Gooch scored 333 at Lord's.
PETER EDWARDS, Chief Executive Essex CC, after above statement, 1993

I turned to God at sea; I prayed every day. Never on land. You know how insignificant you are at sea; on land it seems to matter that you change your car every year.
CHAY BLYTH, British yachtsman, 1974

As flies to wanton boys, are we to the gods;
They kill us for their sport.
Lear in SHAKESPEARE, *King Lear*, 1604

Cricket is a game invented by the British who, not being a spiritual people, had to have some concept of eternity.
MAHARAJA OF BARODA, 1930s

32

Injuries

I am still badly feeling the effect of my injury and will not be returning to the Yorkshire side for some time.
Cricketer GEOFFREY BOYCOTT after scoring 138 not out in a club match for Leeds, 1971

Wouldn't it make more sense if I just got in the fridge?
QASIM OMAR, Pakistan cricketer, who needed six icepacks on wounds inflicted by Australia's bowlers, 1983

It's a tired athlete who gets injured.
DR KEN KINGSBURY, specialist in sports medicine, 1989

There's more ice in there than sank the *Bismarck*.
GERRY FRANCIS, English football manager, after visiting dressing room, 1992

The average lifespan or mortality rate of a professional football player who has played four or more years in the NFL has ranged between 54 and 58, which, in my opinion, speaks for the cumulative effect of the damage and the lifestyle that the game and the pressure of the game puts on the players.
STEVE COURSON, US footballer, 1992

My problem was, I could not say 'no' to my coach.
YELENA MUKHINA, Russian gymnast who broke her neck training for the 1980 Olympic Games, 1992

I wouldn't wish injury on anyone, but you don't really know what the game's all about until you've experienced it.

When I look back I can see that I've paid the price for chasing world records for the last four years.
STEVE BACKLEY, British world record javelin thrower, 1993

I've had about ten operations. I'm a bit like a battered old Escort. You might find one panel left that's original.

I've got scar tissue on scar tissue. My back, my knees, my wrists. My face has been so caved in it has needed a crowbar to straighten it out. I've got so much metal in me I set off airport metal detectors. I don't want to be arthritic at the age of 45. I want to enjoy my life with my family.
English cricketer IAN BOTHAM on his retirement, 1993

It's like a car. There was a mechanical failure and that was it.
DALEY THOMPSON, British athlete, after limping off the Crystal Palace track after failing a fitness test for the Olympic Games, 1992

John Barnes' problem is that he gets injured appearing on *Question of Sport*.
TOMMY DOCHERTY, football manager, 1993

When I saw my face I looked like Elephant Man.

This is not a normal injury. Fashanu was playing without due care and attention.
GARY MABBUTT, Tottenham Hotspur footballer, after a clash with John Fashanu of Wimbledon, 1993

I was not booked over the Gary Mabbutt incident and I will be playing in just the same style. I am a senior professional, and I've been in the game 17 years.
JOHN FASHANU, 1993

Tottenham may be upset but surely it's the same as a car accident. You always think the other driver is to blame.
JOHN DAVEY of the FA committee of inquiry which exonerated Fashanu of blame over the incident, 1993

When you throw your elbows out like that, you are going to hit somebody. He was not going up like that for his own protection.
KEVIN MORAN, Blackburn Rovers FC, whose nose was broken in collision with John Fashanu's elbow in January 1993

They say injuries come in threes. In my case it seems to be thirty threes.
PAUL GASCOIGNE, footballer (England and Italy), November 1993

33

Leadership

It is a fine thing to command, even if it be only a herd of cattle.
MIGUEL DE CERVANTES (1547–1616), Spanish novelist, author of
Don Quixote

If the blind lead the blind, both shall fall into the ditch.
The Bible, Matthew 15:14

Reason and judgement are the qualities of a leader.
TACITUS (*c.* AD 55–120), Roman historian

I must follow them. I am their leader.
British Prime Minister A. BONAR LAW (1858–1923), 1922

Take all the credit you can for victory, in the sure and certain knowledge that you will be given all the blame in defeat.
RICHIE BENAUD, Australian cricketer and commentator

There are a few people in rugby who will gloat over an England
defeat, especially if it involves the fall of Carling. He attracts the
green-eyed monster in many.
SIMON BARNES, journalist, *The Times*, 1993

I've never heard so many swear words in one sentence that made so
much sense.
MIKE BAILEY, Preston Grasshoppers RFC, on what captain Wade
Dooley had said to inspire his team at half time; they won 16–13,
after being 0–13 down, 1992

There are times, even now, when reticence overtakes him; many an
England captain, now forgotten, could teach him a thing or two about
collecting champagne. But few England captains can ever have played
a braver, more resolute innings than we saw from Gooch this week-
end. You can see how much his team wants to play for him. Like every

outstanding captain, he contrives by sheer force of example to make a team into more than the sum of its parts.
The *Guardian* leader, June 1991, after Gooch had led England to the first victory over West Indies at home since 1969

Gooch is only a little lower than the angels.
JOHN WOODCOCK, journalist, *The Times*, June 1991

He has managed to persuade the players they are capable of winning, supremely important in a game so dominated by psychology.
The Times leader, about Graham Gooch, June 1991

Time to Texa-Go, Goochie.

Graham Gooch must swallow his pride and quit as England captain.
Sun headline after England's 3–0 defeat in Texaco Cup, 24 May 1993

Keith Fletcher always said I was a hopeless tosser.
GRAHAM GOOCH after losing toss and First Test to Australia, 1993

There'll be another England captain in the next Test. ... [The side needs] fresh ideas, a fresh approach, someone fresh to look up to. It's right and proper someone else should have a go.
GRAHAM GOOCH resigning the captaincy, 26 July 1993

I don't think it's any coincidence that great captains have been the ones with great teams.
BOBBY SIMPSON, Australian cricket manager, 1993

Unlike his footballing counterpart, whose main duties are to call the toss and offer loud encouragement, a cricket captain must be permanently alert. Cricket presents tactical complexities undreamt of on the football pitch; it is chess compared to tiddlywinks.
The Times leader on the England cricket captaincy, 1993

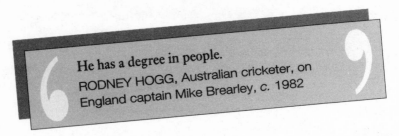

He has a degree in people.
RODNEY HOGG, Australian cricketer, on
England captain Mike Brearley, *c.* 1982

He is also a gentleman. His appointment in many ways heralds a return to the days when cricket was the preserve of amateurs. Apart from being a genuine Test player, he should also be an accomplished after-dinner speaker, an astute tactician, a master diplomat, a rugged fighter, an outstanding press liaison officer, an inspiration to those he commands and a passionate lover of the game.
TREVOR BAILEY, former England all-rounder and BBC commentator, on the England cricket captaincy, 1993

Captaincy is about how well the other guys play around you, and having a good bit of luck.
ALLAN BORDER, Australian Test cricket captain, 1993

I was a bit reluctant. I'd always been one of the boys and suddenly, I was in charge. There are expectations placed on a captain and it is a lot harder than people think. You tend to ride every ball bowled and get mentally exhausted far quicker. ... I always got a good response from the players but it was not until the 1989 Ashes tour that I got to grips with it.
ALLAN BORDER, reflecting in 1993 on getting the captaincy, in 1984

What angered me most was the leadership issue. All along I considered the two of us equals. You cannot possibly have a leader in a two-man venture, the idea is completely daft. But Ran insisted on making a big thing out of being in charge and there were times I could have killed him for it.
DR MIKE STROUD, *Shadows on the Wasteland*, on the first unaided trek across the Antarctic which he made with Sir Ranulph Fiennes, 1993

Any player in the team talk can suggest ideas or changes. . . . But few of them do today. But Danny, he always did. He was a good captain and I backed to the hilt any decision he took on the field. Since Danny went, I've never been able to talk as well to anyone about the team. I miss that.
Spurs manager BILL NICHOLSON about Danny Blanchflower, quoted in Hunter Davies, *The Glory Game*, 1972

He was our captain – and always will be.
BILLY BINGHAM, Northern Ireland football manager, on Danny Blanchflower, at his funeral, December 1993

I'd have run through that door for him. I still would. And he knew that.
MICK McCARTHY, football manager, reflecting on his international career under Jack Charlton, 1994

John Hollins was a mistake. He has a very strong wife. It might have been better if I'd made her manager.
KEN BATES, football club chairman, on managers he has fired, 1994

I don't think people have any idea of the pressures involved. Being captain of a losing side in a country starved of international success has been a nightmare.

I know I will be called a rat and a quitter. That's nothing new because I have become more accustomed to abuse rather than support. I just don't think I can take another three months of the intense pressure.
PAUL THORBURN, Welsh rugby union captain, on resigning from international rugby, August 1991

Before it happened I could see ten years ahead, ten years at the top. After it, I had two choices, either to lie down and hide, or pick up the challenge. My wife Jean and the people of Manchester made the decision for me.
SIR MATT BUSBY (1909–94), reflecting in 1983 (in interview with Rob Hughes, English journalist) on the Munich air disaster 1957

34

Leisure

Increased means and increased leisure are the two civilizers of mankind.
BENJAMIN DISRAELI (1804–81), British statesman

The end of labour is to gain leisure.
ARISTOTLE (384–322 BC), Greek philosopher and scientist

A perpetual holiday is a good working description of Hell.
GEORGE BERNARD SHAW (1856–1950), Irish dramatist

Leisure consists in all those virtous activities by which a man grows morally, intellectually and spiritually. It is that which makes a life worth living.
CICERO (106–43 BC), Roman statesman and writer

Public money is scarcely ever so well employed as in securing bits of waste ground and keeping them as open space.
SIR ARTHUR HELPS (1813–75), English author

It should be noted that children's games are not merely games; one should regard them as their most serious activities.
MICHEL DE MONTAIGNE (1533–92), French essayist

The leisure problem is fundamental. Having to decide what we do with our leisure is inevitably forcing us to re-examine the purpose of human existence, and to ask what human fulfilment really means.
JULIAN HUXLEY (1887–1975), English scientist, *Bulletin of Atomic Scientists*

Many people suffer from a lingering feeling that leisure is something of a luxury ... when carried to excess it is called idleness. But the Committee believe that it is time for the puritan view of leisure to be jettisoned. Leisure is as much a part of life as work and it plays an equally important part in man's development and the quality of his life ... in its own way it is almost as important to the wellbeing of the community as good housing, hospitals and schools.
Report by Select Committee of the House of Lords, 1973

Footballers tend not to notice or enjoy what's around them. I remember once on a tour of Italy the coach passed the Leaning Tower of Pisa. I pointed it out, only to be told, 'Shut up and deal'.
BOBBY CHARLTON, English footballer, 1985

Play so you can be serious.
ARISTOTLE (384–322 BC), Greek philosopher and scientist

As for the darts team, it is not true to say that there will be no welcome for them – they are valued customers of many years' standing. However, it is true to say that there will be no dartboard on the premises after the alterations.
Stockport Messenger, newspaper, 1982

For what do we live, but to make sport for our neighbours, and laugh at them in our turn?
JANE AUSTEN (1775–1817), English novelist, in *Pride and Prejudice*, 1813

We are closer to the ants than to the butterflies. Very few people can endure much leisure.
GERALD BRENAN (1894–1987), British writer, in *Thoughts in a Dry Season*, 1978

I'll be at your Board, when at leisure from cricket.
JOHN MONTAGU, Earl of Sandwich (1718–92), on being appointed a Lord Commissioner of the Admiralty, 1745

Personally, I look upon cricket as organized loafing.
WILLIAM TEMPLE (1881–1944), Archbishop of Canterbury

It is all work and no play in the brain department that makes John Bull such an uncommonly dull boy.
GEORGE BERNARD SHAW (1856–1950), Irish dramatist, in *Music in London 1890–94*, 1932

Done the elephants, done the poverty, nothing left to do.
PHIL TUFNELL, England cricketer, during tour of India, 1993

Visiting a prostitute is in the same league as fishing or football as a leisure activity.
HILARY KINNELL, Birmingham Research Project, 1993

We went to opera and football before I was in politics and I intend to keep doing so – it beats reading White Papers.
Prime Minister JOHN MAJOR, 1992

Oh, for the cricket field!
Former Prime Minister, SIR ALEX DOUGLAS HOME, in a letter to a friend during the 1960s

35

Losing

It needs more skill than I can tell
To play the second fiddle well.
C. H. SPURGEON (1834–92), English preacher

We are not interested in the possibilities of defeat.
QUEEN VICTORIA (1819–1901)

One of the first businesses of a sensible man is to know when he is
beaten, and to leave off fighting at once.
SAMUEL BUTLER (1835–1902), English writer

There's no excuse for happy losers.
BILLY MARTIN, New York Yankees baseball manager

We'll put that medal in a bottom drawer – if we don't throw it away.
PETER COE, athletics coach, on the Silver medal won by his son
Sebastian in the Moscow Olympic 800 metres, 1980

One and three-quarter minutes of total disaster. That was the one I
came for.
SEBASTIAN COE, British athlete, 1980, on the same race

Positive results in sport are magnified, but so are negative results.
Failure breeds failure.
SEBASTIAN COE, 1984

He rode well. I wish he'd fallen off though.
LESTER PIGGOTT, English jockey, after finishing second, 1991

Losing still hurts, but that's good. When it stops hurting, that's when
I stop playing.
MARTINA NAVRATILOVA, US tennis player, 1989

It was like being run over by a truck.
MARTINA NAVRATILOVA after defeat by Monica Seles, 1992

He should come back. The Americans love beating up old Frank.
US boxer MIKE TYSON on Frank Bruno, 1991

The pockets looked like a mouse's ear and the balls as though they had a quarter of a mile to travel.
JOHN VIRGO, snooker player, 1991

You can glory in a team triumphant, but you fall in love with a team in defeat.
ROGER KAHN, on the Brooklyn Dodgers, in *The Boys of Summer*, 1972

It doesn't matter if you win or lose until you lose.
MARTIN PIPE, horse racing trainer, 1993

I have always felt that if you come close enough, one day has to be your day. But if it never happens, it's not the end of the world. People say you can't be called a great player without winning Wimbledon. Was Ken Rosewall a great player? He never won it either.
IVAN LENDL, US tennis player 1992

I haven't lost a war. No one got killed. I just lost a tennis match.
BORIS BECKER, German tennis player, after losing in second round at Wimbledon, as defending champion, 1987

The confidence you lose in defeat is out of all proportion to the confidence you gain from a victory. You gain it in inches and you lose it in yards.
HOWARD WILKINSON, Leeds United manager, January 1993

Now I am not playing like I used to and everywhere I go, at the bar, in the hotel, every press centre, I get the same questions all the time. I feel like I have committed a crime, like I have done something very bad, but all I can say is ... I'm not playing very well, that's all.
SEVERIANO BALLESTEROS, Spanish golfer, August 1993

Of all the teams in the world you don't want to lose to, England's top of the list. The English know no humility in victory or defeat. ... If you beat them, it's because you cheat. If they beat you, it's because they've overcome your cheating. Good teams learn how to win and lose with graciousness and humility. England hasn't learned that lesson yet.
GRANT FOX, New Zealand rugby union player, following remarks about All Black behaviour on tour of Britain, December 1993

The whole of our national sport is not doing very well. We may be in the wrong sign or something. Venus may be in the wrong juxtaposition to something.
TED DEXTER, Chairman of the Cricket Selection Committee, commenting on England's losing run, June 1993

I'm not aware of any mistakes I've made.
TED DEXTER after 4–0 defeat by Australia, 1989

Relegation is the devil of the game. And if you did away with the devil, life would be pretty boring.
DANNY BLANCHFLOWER (1926–93), Tottenham Hotspur and Northern Ireland footballer

In Wales the half backs, especially the stand off half, always get the blame.
NEIL JENKINS, rugby union player, January 1993

Wembley ... is a wonderful, wonderful place, the best in the world when you win. But when you lose, it looks dirty and empty.
OSVALDO ARDILES, West Bromwich Albion FC manager, after winning second division play-offs v. Port Vale, May 1993

I cried in the locker room. And Seve Ballesteros cried with me.
CONSTANTINO ROCCA, whose defeat in the 1993 Ryder Cup singles meant that Europe lost to the USA

The world is made of people who never quite get into the first team and who just miss the prizes at the flower show.
JACOB BRONOWSKI (1908–74), British scientist and writer

36

Luck

When God throws the dice are loaded.
Greek proverb

Unseen, in the background, Fate was quietly slipping the lead into the boxing glove.
P. G. WODEHOUSE (1881–1975), English writer and humourist,
Very Good Jeeves, 1930

I believe in God. I don't believe in fortune.
AYRTON SENNA (1960–94), Brazilian motor racing driver, 1993

Chance is a word that does not make sense. Nothing happens without a cause.
VOLTAIRE (1694–1778), French writer

Destiny plays a big part in everyone's life. You play golf, you play good, you hit a good drive at the last hole and it is in a divot hole in the middle of the fairway. That has to be destiny.
SEVERIANO BALLESTEROS, Spanish golfer, 1993

Of course I don't believe in it. But I understand that it brings you luck whether you believe in it or not.
NIELS BOHR (1885–1962), Danish physicist, when asked why he had a horseshoe on his wall.

See, you do your best. And it's only a game, that's all. But these days you just can't lose. There's got to be reasons, it's got to be someone's fault. Now sport doesn't work like that. Sometimes, it's just a matter of luck, nothing more. But you try coming out with that line when England have lost at cricket or football.
GRAHAM GOOCH, English cricketer, reflecting on Graham Taylor and the management/leadership of England football or cricket, 1993

37

Management

Being a manager is simple. All you have to do is keep the five players who hate your guts away from the five who are undecided.
CASEY STENGEL (1891–1975), US ex-baseball manager, 1974

I don't want any yes men around me. I want everybody to tell me the truth even if it costs them their jobs.
SAMUEL GOLDWYN (1882–1974), US film producer

Whether you are an experienced international, with lots of games behind you, or a young boy with none, you sometimes need a cuddle.
GRAHAM TAYLOR, England football manager (on John Barnes, in particular), 1993

As a player I could find consolation in defeat, if I'd had a good game. For a manager, there's no consolation. You just lose.
STEVE COPPELL, football manager, 1993

A lot of people were surprised I even had a heart.
MIKE DITKA, Chicago Bears football team coach, after heart attack, 1988

I'm a people's man. Only the people matter.
BILL SHANKLY (1913–81), football manager

I had never been in the situation of running a rugby team but I had been in the situation of controlling 30 players on a rugby field and trying to get those players to perform to the best of their abilities, and that's man management. There are a lot of coaches in Wales with a far better knowledge of scrummaging technique and of three quarter play than myself but, hopefully, I can manage well. That's all it is, man management.
CLIVE NORLING, Bridgend Rugby Football Club (and former international rugby referee), 1993

The longer you stay in the game, the further you grow away from it.
JOE MERCER (1914–90), English footballer and manager (including of the England team)

There's no real gratitude.
BILL SHANKLY (1913–81), after retiring from Liverpool FC

The two things you can't give anybody in this game are bravery and enthusiasm.

Football is my hobby. I like footballers who are equally keen. I tell my players – don't bore me.
RON ATKINSON, English football manager, 1993

One morning at training Clough says, 'Right, tracksuit bottoms off, run in and out of there', pointing to a field of nettles. We were stung to high heaven but we all went.
VIV ANDERSON, English footballer, 1988

It's a great job, apart from Saturday afternoons.
JOCKY SCOTT, Dunfermline Athletic FC manager, then bottom of Scottish Premier Division, 1991

If I wasn't the manager, I would have gone home early.
ALEX MILLER, Hibernian FC manager, 1991

The only certainty about management is the sack.
JOHNNY GILES, footballer and football manager

I like to think I am fair. But in football management you can't be fair
all the time because the job doesn't entail that. The specifics of the job
are that you have to be unfair, you have to lie and cheat.
TERRY BUTCHER, English footballer and manager, 1994

I'm pleased for him but it's like watching your mother-in-law drive
off the cliff in your new car.
TERRY VENABLES, chief executive of Tottenham Hotspur FC, after
transferring Paul Gascoigne to Italy, 1992

They've called me a one-horse trainer but at least I made a bloody
good job of the one horse I got.
GINGER McCAIN, trainer of Red Rum, 1992

He treats us like men. He lets us wear earrings.
TORRIN POLK, University of Houston footballer, on coach
J. Jenkins, *c.* 1990

When you're manager of a football club the players are your children.
ARTHUR COX, English football manager, 1993

People go to rugby league to be emotional, I go to rugby league to
work.
JOHN MONIE, Wigan rugby league coach, after his last game, the
Premiership final v. St Helens, 1993

Money 1, Football 0.
Cardboard sign on Tottenham Hotspur's gates after sacking of
Terry Venables, Chief Executive, 1993

I've been made to feel like the man who shot Bambi.
ALAN SUGAR, businessman (Chairman and founder of Amstrad),
majority shareholder in Tottenham Hotspur FC, in first comments
about his sacking of Terry Venables as chief executive, 1993

I feel like Robin Hood – feared by the bad, loved by the good.
TERRY VENABLES, 1993

We didn't actually have to get on. I would run the company and keep him in touch with what was going on and he would run the board meetings and make his presence felt there. But really it wasn't us going out dancing together. It was a working relationship.
TERRY VENABLES reflecting on being sacked by Alan Sugar, and after a High Court hearing had given him temporary reinstatement, 1993

This famous football club is bigger than any one man – and that includes Terry Venables.
ALAN SUGAR, 1993

I had everything going for me as a player. I had good control and I could run, but the most important thing is to have a football brain. If you have got a good football brain but you are one-paced or your feet are not quick enough, as Ron (Atkinson) may have been, that will stop you from being a player, but it won't stop you from being a manager.
ALAN BALL, English footballer and manager, 1994

Personality must be the key factor in managerial success. It is not a question of being a nice man or a nasty one, of being likeable or aloof, or being imaginative or cautious, hard or indulgent in discipline. All of these things are subordinate to the essential quality – the capacity to dominate. He is the kind of man who will not permit interference from amateurs, and the kind who will never be invited to work for a board nor prepared to be overshadowed.
ARTHUR HOPCROFT, English writer and journalist, *The Football Man*, 1971

The letters say, 'You should have sold him, him and him and bought him, him and him.' These people think it's like selling ashtrays.
HOWARD WILKINSON, Leeds United FC manager, on the hate mail he received during the 1992/3 season's disappointing league campaign, 1993

The beauty of Cup football is that Jack always had a chance of beating Goliath.
TERRY BUTCHER, then Sunderland FC manager, before a Cup match v. Leeds, 1993

The trouble with senior management to an outsider is that there are too many one ulcer men holding down two ulcer men's jobs.
HRH DUKE OF EDINBURGH

If it's my best friend or my biggest enemy, if you don't score enough in his position then you're out. Don't talk about relationships, those are facts.
JOHANN CRUYFF, Dutch footballer and Barcelona manager, *c.* 1990

Problems? You think you've got problems? England are 120 for 9.
KEN TYRRELL, founder in 1963 of Tyrrell Racing, to driver Jackie Stewart, who was complaining about his Grand Prix car

Let us have patience with our inferiors. They are ourselves of yesterday.
ISAAC GOLDBERG (1887–1938), American critic

Look, if you're in the penalty area and aren't quite sure what to do with the ball, just stick it into the net and we'll discuss all your options afterwards.
BILL SHANKLY (1913–81), football manager

Lots of folks confuse bad management with destiny.
KIN (F. McKINNEY) HUBBARD (1868–1930), American humorist/journalist

I've just given our Chairman a vote of confidence.
BRIAN CLOUGH, football manager, 1992

If I had one flaw, it was that I was too trusting.
MIKE TYSON, US boxer, discussing the change of management achieved without his consent, 1991

It's hard to be passionate twice a week.
GEORGE GRAHAM, Arsenal FC manager, on the burden of the fixture list, 1992

I've told the players not to bother winning too much because I won't be able to stand the pressure.
DENNIS SMITH, Sunderland FC manager, after resignation of Kenny Dalglish as Liverpool manager, 1991

I've given you the facts, but they might not be the true facts.
ALEX FERGUSON, Manchester United FC manager, fending off
questions about injury fears for defender Pallister, 1992

There is a rat in the camp trying to throw a spanner in the works.
CHRIS CATTLIN, Brighton football manager, 1983

Those who tell you it is tough at the top have never been at the
bottom.
JOE HARVEY, Newcastle United FC manager, 1973

There's no fun in soccer anymore. It's all deadly serious. We'll end up
playing in cemeteries.
TERRY VENABLES, English football manager, 1973

As a manager you're like a prostitute. You depend on other people for
your living.
STEVE COPPELL, English football manager, 1993

1983, with Charlton. . . . A transfer embargo, no players and about to
get liquidated at any time. THAT was pressure.
Manager LENNIE LAWRENCE on soccer relegation battles, 1993

The big clubs have got about ten points advantage right from the start
and they also get the decisions, the free kicks and the praise.
DAVE BASSETT, Sheffield United FC manager, 1993

If they finish second they've flopped.
RON ATKINSON, football manager, on Manchester United FC,
1993

It's the sort of place you get into as late as possible, bring your own
grub, go to bed, get up, play the game and get out.
JACK CHARLTON, Eire football manager, after a fact-finding trip to
Tirana, Albania, 1993

I can count on the fingers of one hand ten games where we've caused
our own downfall.
JOE KINNEAR, Wimbledon FC manager, 1993

38

Media

At its best, sport is a living drama.
JOHN BROMLEY, OBE, ITV Head of Sport, 1982

We work in the toy department.

A rabid sports fan is one who boos a TV set.
JIMMY CANNON (1910–73), US sportswriter

The sports page records people's accomplishments; the front page has nothing but man's failures.
JUDGE EARL WARREN (1891–1974), Governor of California

Television has democratized the enjoyment of sport.
Economist, January 1988

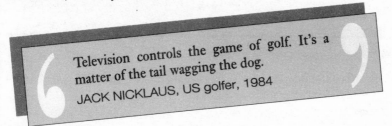

Television controls the game of golf. It's a matter of the tail wagging the dog.
JACK NICKLAUS, US golfer, 1984

The mission of a modern newspaper is to comfort the afflicted and afflict the comfortable.
ANON

Give someone half a page in a newspaper and they think they own the world.
JEFFREY BARNARD, British journalist, 1992

Doctors bury their mistakes. Lawyers hang them. Journalists put theirs on the front page.
ANON

I've got a face made for radio.
RON LUCIANO, US baseball umpire, on his failure as NBC TV
summarizer, 1984

Journalism is still an underdeveloped profession and, accordingly,
newspapermen are quite often regarded as were surgeons and mus-
cians a century ago, as having the rank, roughly speaking, of barbers
and riding masters.
WALTER LIPPMANN (1889–1974), US journalist

Would it be too much to ask my old TV colleague Geoffrey Boycott,
whose knowledge of cricket is profound, and whose comments are so
often illuminating, to pause for breath now and again and ease up on
the tutorial?
PETER WEST, English journalist and commentator, in letter to *The
Times*, after one-day cricket series England v. West Indies, 1991

Sports are the greatest thing that's ever happened to TV, the only
honest thing that goes on. And I don't just say that because we have
the field surrounded. As the overall quality of TV begins to deterio-
rate, sports will become even more effective. There's no such thing as
too much sport on TV.
BARRY FRANK, Vice President of International Management Group
(IMG), 1975

I hate this attitude the media have that just because someone is good
at sport means that their opinion on any topic is of fantastic importance.
STEVE OVETT, British athlete, *c.* 1985

If baseball was half as complicated as some of the writers make out it
is, a lot of us boys from the farm would never have been able to make a
living out of it.
WILLIAM 'BUCKY' WALTERS (born 1909), Boston Red Sox,
Cincinnati Reds

The difference between us is that your teams never actually have to
play.
GRAHAM TAYLOR, England football manager to football writers at
Press Conference, 1993

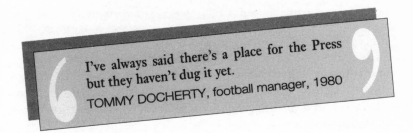

I've always said there's a place for the Press but they haven't dug it yet.
TOMMY DOCHERTY, football manager, 1980

We certainly wouldn't accept a contract with a governing body that allowed them any editorial control of our programming.
JONATHAN MARTIN, BBC Head of Sport, 1992

Criticism is a fact of life, it's not new – players in all countries experience it. Unless you win every game as an international player, it'll always be there, but it doesn't help, particularly when it's specific and personal stuff.
MICHAEL BRADLEY, Ireland rugby union captain, 1994

I would have gone to a tabloid newspaper and, for thousands of pounds, said that I did it. But I wouldn't do that, not for £1 million, because I want to prove that I didn't take drugs.
JASON LIVINGSTONE, British athlete, 1992

Cricket is the national game and the BBC is the national broadcasting channel. It ought to be part of its duty, as a public body receiving public funds, to provide proper coverage of national sports teams. Instead, it is sulking in its tent at the viewers' expense. Not the right way to win friends and influence people, least of all a cricket-loving Prime Minister.
Letter to the *Guardian*, on BBC's failure to provide other than news coverage (2 minutes) of England tour of India, covered by BSkyB satellite TV, 1993

I would prefer to keep all sports pure, but the fact of the matter is that, depending on how much you have at risk to televise the match depends on how much you need to modify the sport, to accommodate the messages. That's how the business is based.
STEVE BORNSTEIN, ESPN, 1992

I would like to thank the press from the heart of my bottom.
British golfer NICK FALDO after winning the British Open, 1992

We have now reached a stage where sport at top level has become almost completely show business with everything that one associates with show biz: the cult of the individual, high salaries, the desire to present a game as a spectacle – with more money, less sportsmanship, more emphasis on winning. All this has come about through television.
SIR DENNIS FOLLOWS, Chairman of the British Olympic Association, 1983

If you don't know [them] then you don't know what's behind their ... event, or the athletic prowess in that individual sport. What we have to do is inform ... and then you can live and breathe with those people's ups and downs *and* their careers.

Television has brought dollar signs to sport more than anything else.
ROSS GREENBERG, Home Box Office (US cable network), 1992

I remember that [Steve Ovett] used to bring an alarm clock on to the track with him as his form of protest!
British athlete SEBASTIAN COE on the late races put on to suit TV times, 1992

The live events ... happened early in the morning, 9.30 a.m., but people were not in the stands yet. In America they thought if people have not bothered to sit and watch this event, maybe it's not important enough.
ALEX GILLARDI, NBC, on perceived reductions in Seoul Olympics' TV audiences, 1992

We shouldn't be in a position where we affect what's happening on the playing field. ... But TV is the bread and butter of sport ... We're pumping a lot of money into production costs. Because of that there are certain considerations we would expect.
DONALD COLANTONIO, American TV company ESPN, 1992

[The process is] a food chain – TV feeds the sponsors and sponsors feed the event organisers.
DONALD COLANTONIO, ESPN, 1992

If you don't bid for the Olympics you make more money for sure than if you do bid for the Olympics. But the Games are just before the start of the [new Autumn] season. It should attract good ratings and thus catch audiences and advertisers for later programmes. It is something of a loss leader.
ALEX GILLARDI, NBC, 1992

From Mount Olympus to Tampa Stadium is a long journey ... the invention has taken over the inventor; a real-life Frankenstein indeed.
JONATHAN RENDALL, journalist, after US Superbowl at Tampa in 1991

When he was rugby football correspondent of *The Times*, the late V. A. Titley declined to use the first names of players in his reports since in most cases he had not been introduced to them.
GEOFFREY NICHOLSON, British journalist, 1979

I'll speak for the same length of time as the average English batsman lasted at the crease in India – five seconds.
JONATHAN AGNEW, accepting the award of Sports Reporter of the Year 1993, at the Sony Radio Awards

La Gazzetta [*dello Sport*] is not only the most important sports daily in the world, but it is the one to tell us, day after day, how to act and what to do.
JUAN ANTONIO SAMARANCH, President of the IOC, during Barcelona Games, 1992; reported in the *Guardian*, 1993

I believe 75 per cent of the media dislike us. We are liked by maybe 25 per cent. Even though, when we won the title under my management, we played stylish, attractive football. Other southern clubs are struggling, but we are the ones taking the stick.
GEORGE GRAHAM, Arsenal FC manager, December 1993

Within the England squad we have totally outlawed the tabloid stuff.
TED DEXTER, Chairman of the Cricket Selection Committee, June 1993

I don't read it. It seems to me to have nothing to do with the job that I'm supposed to do. It's absolutely incidental.
TED DEXTER, also in June 1993, when asked about press criticism

He did brilliantly with the team, on and off the field, he batted well and he was good with the Press. I couldn't give him higher praise.
KEITH FLETCHER, team manager, on new England cricket captain Mike Atherton after his first Test, which was lost, 1993

Just when he thought it couldn't get much worse. England cricket captain Mike Atherton's girl has dumped him. Just as well she hasn't given him her heart. He would only have dropped it.
Sun leader, April 1994

Good pros deserve good prose.
ANDREW ANTHONY, journalist, the *Guardian*, August 1991

Blood sport is brought to its ultimate refinement in the gossip columns.
SIR BERNARD INGHAM, Press Secretary to Prime Minister Margaret Thatcher, December 1986

Somewhere along the line did I give you the impression I care what you think?
US tennis player ANDRE AGASSI addressing a journalist at a press conference, 1993

A good newspaper, I suppose, is a nation talking to itself.
ARTHUR MILLER, US dramatist, November 1961

A critic is a legless man who teaches running.
ANON

A drama critic is a man who leaves no turn unstoned.
GEORGE BERNARD SHAW (1856–1950), Irish dramatist, *New York Times*, November 1950

It's a very privileged and nice thing to be a journalist and journalists should check the facts.
ELTON JOHN, entertainer, after winning £350 000 in libel damages from the *Sunday Mirror*, 1993

Basically he is happy with what he has done.
MAX CLIFFORD, PR specialist, on behalf of Bryce Taylor who took photos secretly of the Princess of Wales while she was working out in his gym, 1993

It's not my favourite subject, it never has been. It's your favourite subject.
GRAHAM TAYLOR, England football manager, faced with the usual barrage of media questions about Paul Gascoigne, 1993

When I give an interview, the quotes that are used aren't the ones that I would like them to use. They need something sensational, at all costs. ... It's nothing though compared to what's written about Gascoigne.
ERIC CANTONA, French footballer, 1993

I am not the editor of a newspaper and shall always try to do right and be good so that God will not make me one.
MARK TWAIN (1835–1910), US writer and wit

39

Men and Women

Women never look so well as when one comes in wet and dirty from hunting.
ROBERT SURTEES (1803–64), English writer, *Mr Sponge's Sporting Tour*, 1853

'After all, golf is only a game', said Millicent.
Women say these things without thinking. It does not mean there is any kink in their character. They simply don't think what they are saying.
P. G. WODEHOUSE (1881–1975), English writer and humorist, in *The Clicking of Cuthbert*, 1922

Lord Hawke probably took the same view as I do about families on tour with the MCC players. It is no more a place for them than a trench on the Somme.
JOHN WOODCOCK, *The Times* cricket correspondent, 1975

> Professionalism is, if you like, not having sex on Thursdays and Fridays.
> DON REVIE, England football manager, 1976

I've nothing against letting wives into the team camp. Sex is good for footballers, so long as it is not at half time.
RICHARD MOELLER NIELSEN, manager of European soccer champions, Denmark, 1992

When we were living in Sydney, a friend told me that one night, while she and her husband were making love, she suddenly noticed something sticking in his ear. When she asked him what it was he replied, 'Be quiet! I'm listening to the cricket!'
VICKY RANTZEN, *Observer*, 1978

We hope to revive the old tradition of the husband going to football on Xmas Day while the wife cooks the turkey.
Official of Brentford FC, 1983

'Mortimer, you must choose between golf and me'.
'But darling, I went round in 101 yesterday. You can't expect a fellow to give up golf when he's at the top of his game'.
P. G. WODEHOUSE, *The Clicking of Cuthbert*, 1922

For the Davis Cup you have to have separate bedrooms from your husband while he is training. You spend the whole of the year living with him then all of a sudden they say, 'No, no, naughty, not the night before the Davis Cup'. I suppose it's because they are representing England.
MRS MARK COX, wife of the British tennis player Mark Cox, 1971

No man is fit to be called a sportsman what doesn't kick his wife out of bed on an average once in three weeks.
ROBERT SURTEES (1803–64), English writer

Anyone who knows Dan Quayle knows he would rather play golf than have sex any day.
MRS QUAYLE, wife of the then US Vice President, 1992

I know about women and they're more dangerous than fighting.
LENNOX LEWIS, heavyweight boxing champion, 1992

I used to be with three women until 5 a.m. Now I'm in training, it's five women until 3 a.m.
ALBERTO TOMBA, Italian skier, 1992

A runner runs best when he or she has a good, steady background. Having a happy sex life and a supportive partner helps to make a successful runner. However, I can see that some people will only produce their best when they are feeling angry or frustrated.
BRUCE TULLOH, British runner, 1994

They are too young. A 20 year-old is like a rising sun. So they have to be this way to have their career.
MA JUNREN, Chinese athletics coach, explaining why his charges are not allowed romances, January 1994

Girls are a distraction and can easily cost points.
BORIS BECKER, German tennis player, 1986

Sex gets in the way of winning.
JIM COURIER, US tennis player, explaining break-up with girlfriend,
1992

I always knew I would have boys. No one could ever convince me
there was a possibility that I was going to have girls ... there was just
no way I could have produced girls. I'm a man and I would only produce a man child.
CHRIS EUBANK, British boxer, 1992

You would think this England Test team was in a holiday camp. Their
dining room has high chairs for the players' children and on morn-
ings of tough Tests England's heroes are popping cornflakes into their
children's mouths. In Brisbane or Sydney it was absurd to call these
men with bats, batsmen; they were weak-kneed imposters.
KEITH MILLER, Australian cricketer and journalist, 1974

I don't want to see knitting needles in the Pavilion.
MARTIN WOOD, MCC member, before vote on women members,
1992

Only women and horses work for nothing.
DOUG ELLIS, Aston Villa's first paid director, 1983

A lot of beautiful girls may be made available to you after the game.
Such traps are aimed at destabilising you. You are going to war and
must be on the lookout for all kinds of weapons.
KING MTETWA, Swaziland Home Affairs Minister, speaking to
Highlanders FC players before match in Lesotho, 1985

When women kiss, it always reminds me of prizefighters shaking
hands.
H. L. MENCKEN (1880–1956), US journalist

I confess I did my best to accommodate as many women as I could.
'MAGIC' JOHNSON, US basketball player, 1992

They'd say, I'm gay, I had it coming.
MARTINA NAVRATILOVA, US tennis player, on public reaction if
she were to get AIDS, 1992

Almost all sport, whether contact or non-contact, is segregated by
gender to the disadvantage of women qualified by their skill to compete with men.
Pannick Report on sex discrimination, 1983

There was this tremendous fear that women would drop dead. We've
had quite a fight.

The Women's Amateur Athletics Association were always able to get
sponsors because all the girls were so pretty. You could put all the athletes I've dealt with on a beauty line. The men weren't so successful
because they weren't so pretty.
MAREA HARTMAN, long-serving Honorary Secretary of British
Women's Amateur Athletic Association (from 1960 to 1991),
reflecting in May 1993 on the campaign to extend the range of
athletics events for women

If women stayed at home and concentrated on the washing and looking after the kids, there would be no problem. I know times have
changed but the situation in bowling clubs hasn't.
BOB YOUNG, President of Scottish Bowling Association, 1992

If a chap wants to go out with a girl after a hard day's cricket, why
not? As long as she's pretty.
TED DEXTER, Chairman of the Cricket Selection Committee, 1992

You can't train the way I do and go out with girls.
JOACHIM CRUZ, Brazilian athlete, 1984

Men kick friendship around like a football, but it doesn't seem to
crack. Women treat it like glass and it goes to pieces.
ANNE MORROW LINDBERGH (born 1906), American writer, poet,
aviator

I never met a man I didn't like.
WILL ROGERS (1879–1935), US humorist

Had Scott of the Antarctic been a woman, he might have made it!
DR CRAIG SHARP, Director of Physiology at the British Olympic
medical centre, arguing that women are better equipped for
endurance events, 1993

If a woman takes the sport more seriously than a hobby, she has to
train harder and that means working only part-time. At that point
most men can get appearance money, enough at least to get by.
Women can't. A woman can be in the top three in her event in the
world and still have to work.
SALLY GUNNELL, British Olympic gold medallist, 1993

There is no doubt in my mind that the break-up of Graham Gooch's
marriage is a significant reason for his lack of form as England's premier batsman and his lack of touch as captain. The pressures on a
celebrity, a public figure with a big following, are much bigger than
those on Mr Average when a marriage breaks up. ... Even I know
what a great cricketer he was when he was a happily married man,
with a wife who loved and supported him. ... The slump in his
cricket seems to have coincided with the slump in his marriage.
MARJORIE PROOPS, *Daily Mirror* 'agony aunt', May 1993

Women can climb as easily as men. It is not a question of strength but
of experience and motivation. There are a lot of men who are stronger
than I am but who don't do what I do. I think of myself as a climbing
machine.
CATHERINE DESTEVILLE, French climber, 1993

When it comes to the crunch, being a woman is not the problem – it is
having the guts.
ANGELA SOPER, former President of the Pinnacle Club, 1993

Growing up in sports as a girl definitely meant being discriminated
against, being discounted because of gender. We were always told we
were worth less.
BILLIE JEAN KING, US tennis player, 1993

I couldn't believe it. The [England] rugby team won only one big match, but we had won the World Cup against all the odds. The BBC only showed a few seconds of the end of the match and didn't even interview us. It's always a problem getting coverage; the Lord's streaker got more footage and column inches than women's cricket got in the last 20 years and that's a symptom of why we find it so hard to be taken seriously.

Blokes still ask us stupid questions like, 'What protection do you wear?' They wouldn't ask Ian Botham that – they would get a fat lip if they did.
CLARE TAYLOR, England cricketer, commenting in December 1993 after BBC's decision to award the Team of the Year Award 1993 to the England rugby union team (for their win over the All Blacks in November)

This is the saddest day of my life. The last time I wore a skirt was 10 years ago!
GLORIA HLALELE, member of South Africa's women's football squad on wearing a new team uniform at a function for the squad on leaving South Africa for Zimbabwe tour, October 1993

Women's rugby is just as aggressive and physical, but there isn't the rough side to it, the going beyond the bounds of the law, that there is in the men's game – thankfully. People say it reminds them of boys of seventeen or eighteen: the love is for the running side of the game. . . . Anyway, I'd argue that men are much more vulnerable to . . . underhand tactics, shall we say?
EMMA MITCHELL, scrum half to England women's rugby union team, December 1993

The margin [in payments] between men and women tennis players at Wimbledon has been narrowed down to about 10 per cent. Yet in athletics the two top champions of our country seem to have a gender difference of 33 per cent.
SALLY GUNNELL, British athlete, 1993

If all the girls here were laid end to end, I wouldn't be at all surprised.
DOROTHY PARKER (1893–1967), US writer and wit

I hate women because they always know where things are.
JAMES THURBER (1894–1961), US humorist

There are a number of mechanical devices which increase sexual arousal in women – one of them is the Mercedes Benz 380SL convertible.
P. J. O'ROURKE (born 1947), US humorist, *c.* 1990

I used to be Snow White but I drifted.
MAE WEST (1893–1980), US actress

Is sex dirty? Only if it's done right.
WOODY ALLEN, US humorist and film director, 1972

A woman's place is in the home.
Proverb (often quoted in sporting circles)

No man can call himself liberal, or radical, or even a conservative advocate of fair play, if his work depends in any way on the unpaid or underpaid labour of women at home, or in the office.
GLORIA STEINMEM, US writer and feminist, *New York Times*, August 1971

God made the woman for the man,
And for the good and increase of the world.
ALFRED LORD TENNYSON (1809–92), English poet, *Edwin Morris*,
1842

Whoever stole it is spending less money than my wife.
ILIE NASTASE, Romanian tennis player, on why he did not report
the loss of his American Express card, 1978

He's now known as Fred Singles.
BERNARD GUIRK, US broadcaster, after golfer Fred Couples'
divorce, May 1993

We would have to extend the regatta to six days. And we find that
after five the lawns are already distressed enough.
MIKE SWEENEY, Chairman of Henley Regatta, explaining why
there is no place for women competitors, 1993

When you look at what men's sport can deliver for the sponsor, there
is no comparison. Men can get recognition for their skill, but for
women, glamour helps. Whether you like it or not, good-looking
women are marketable. It's the old adage of life: women have to promote themselves more than men do.
KAREN EARL, British sponsorship specialist, 1993

The hard core believed that since these girls were rough and ready, so
they must all be lesbians. But the real image of the sport is of intelligent women playing an intelligent sport.
ALICE COOPER, 1993, on attempts to get sponsorship for the
1990 women's rugby World Cup

Thus men may grow wiser every day; it is the first time that I ever
heard breaking of ribs was sport for ladies.
Touchstone in SHAKESPEARE, *As You Like It*, 1599

I have people asking me, 'Aren't you worried about your pretty face?'
Like if I was ugly it wouldn't matter.
DALLAS MOLLOY, who appeared in the first official women's
boxing match in the USA, 1993

40

Modesty

There's only one head bigger than Tony Greig – and that's Birkenhead.
FRED TRUEMAN, English cricketer and commentator, 1975

Rarely can success have gone so little to a man's head. No prima donna posturing for Gooch, his achievement is a triumph of maturity over flashiness, of stolid persistence over erratic brilliance.
The Times leader, June 1991, after England win over West Indies, the first since 1969

The topics that average people talk about are so small and beneath me that I can't handle it.

I'm trying to get into Cambridge University. I want to study psychology. I think I am naturally a master of psychology, but I would like to go into it thoroughly in a recognized way.
CHRIS EUBANK, British boxer, 1992

They wear caps with the same dreadlocks as me, they have their cars sprayed in the colours of my hair and write my name on the side. A picture of my face is on every banner. I've pushed this club to the top. I have been the face of AC Milan over the past four years.
RUUD GULLIT, Dutch footballer, 1992

Brian Clough didn't let me know till the day of the match if I was playing. Then I scored the winning goal and became a household name across Europe.
Footballer TREVOR FRANCIS, when commentating on European Cup Final, 1993, and reflecting on his winning European Cup final for Nottingham Forest FC

Nobody reminds me of me, I'm an original.
JIMMY CONNORS, US tennis player, 1989

In my entire career I have never gone round a golf course and never mishit a shot. Every drive was perfect, every iron was perfect. I was in awe of myself.
Australian golfer GREG NORMAN, after winning British Open, 1993

Even at the summit I felt surprise that Tenzing and myself should have been the lucky ones.
New Zealander SIR EDMUND HILLARY, first conqueror of Everest, reflecting forty years later, 1993

I don't go in too much for nostalgia. Everest was a great experience at the time – but so much has happened since.
SIR EDMUND HILLARY

People just don't like me for the same reason they didn't like Muhammad Ali. We're not quiet, we stand up to be counted. We are the best and we are heard.
DON KING, US boxing promoter, 1993

I'm the best promoter in the world. And I say that humbly.
DON KING, US boxing promoter, 1992

All I needed was a head for heights.
REBECCA STEPHENS, first British woman to climb Everest, May 1993

It's a beautiful city with lovely people. The Trent is lovely, too. I know, I've walked on it for 18 years.
BRIAN CLOUGH, football manager, on receiving the freedom of the City of Nottingham, 1993

When you've won twenty-six world championships, an Olympic medal, four America's Cups and been Yachtsman of the Year seven times, there is not the same urgency to prove your superiority all the time.
DENIS CONNOR, US yachtsman, 1993

Rugby is not all that important to me. I just play for the fun of it. It's not the most vital thing in life, is it?
BARRY JOHN, Wales and British Lions rugby union player, 1971

41

Motivation

Because it's there.
New Zealander GEORGE LEIGH MALLORY (1886–1924), on the reason for trying to climb Everest, *c*. 1920 (understood to be the first time this reason was given)

Some people think football is a matter of life and death. I don't like that attitude. I can assure them it's much more serious than that.
BILL SHANKLY (1913–81), Liverpool FC manager, 1973

It's the thrill of scoring goals that makes me play football. There is nothing like it. It's indescribable ... the emotion of the moment. Satisfaction, joy, occasionally relief. It's everything rolled into one. Just those few seconds of ecstasy.
GARY LINEKER, English footballer, 1991

90 per cent of players are uplifted and perform better by being told they are good players. Only 10 per cent need constantly kicking up the backside.
GARY LINEKER, 1992

The only motivation I needed was to sit in the changing room and tell myself: I'm going to win, I'm going to win.
BRENDON FOSTER, British athlete, 1992

I just told the players to be like cornered tigers, with nowhere to go.
IMRAN KHAN, Pakistani cricket captain, on their victory in the 1992 cricket World Cup after losing their first three matches

If we are due to field, I like to go round each of my players just before we go out. I'll shake hands with each one, wish them luck, and tell them to get stuck in. I look each player straight in the eye, letting them know instinctively what I expect from them. It's a personal gesture from me, a form of bonding, an awareness that it now only involves the eleven of us. I want them to realize that we're doing it for

our country, that we are the honoured ones, this is special, a Test match, the ultimate for any cricketer. I don't want to see anybody slumped in a corner at this time, they should be on a high; I want a buzz of camaraderie. All the hard work, the planning, the talking – it's been channelled into this moment. It's time to go over the top.
GRAHAM GOOCH, England cricket captain, 1992

These English you're just going out to meet have taken our coal, our water, our steel; they buy our houses and only live in them a fortnight a year. . . . Down the centuries these English have exploited and pillaged us – and we're playing them this afternoon, boys.
Part of team talk by PHIL BENNETT, Welsh rugby union captain, before match v. England, 1977

Nothing. I like it when it's over and we got the right result.
PAT JENNINGS, Arsenal and Northern Ireland goalkeeper, when asked what he enjoyed about football

I took up boxing because it was the only way I could see of escaping poverty.
JOHN CONTEH, British boxer, 1981

It was an easy decision to turn pro. I was unemployed.
JOCKY WILSON, Scottish darts player, January 1990

You've just got to pick people and say, 'I believe in you'. And, 'England expects'. All those things. They all get said. And you just hope that two or three people get a gleam in their eye and can take it with them on to the field. . . . Some people take the game on to the field better than others. . . . One or two of them, sadly, leave it behind in the dressing room.
TED DEXTER, Chairman of the Cricket Selection Committee, June 1993

No one can make you feel inferior without your consent.
ELEANOR ROOSEVELT (1884–1962), US humanitarian

To love what you do and feel that it matters – how could anything be more fun?
KATHARINE GRAHAM, US editor and writer, 1974

May the Force be with you.
GEORGE LUCAS, director of *Star Wars* (words spoken by OB1 Kenobi)

Players who look to the bench for their solutions should be on it.
DAVID WHITAKER, Great Britain hockey coach, 1993

But what a feeling when you get one [a winner]. So many of us want to be a Dunwoody, but so few get anywhere near it. What else can I do now? The bad days, when the rain lashes your face, you've just got to take. If you didn't love the sport you'd never stick it.
JASON CLARKE, English stable lad and jockey, 1994

I went 11 games without scoring and Mr Clough came to me and said, 'It's a difficult game, Edward. I know what you're going through. I once went four games myself without scoring'.
TEDDY SHERINGHAM, Spurs footballer, on a pep talk he received when at Nottingham Forest FC, 1993

Ejaculating only costs 60 calories, that's just a chocolate bar.
MARIO CIPOLLINI, Tour de France cyclist, claiming that he would never have raced if the old tradition that cyclists had no sex before a race still prevailed, 1993

If you win, everybody gets to know who you are and that helps to get more girlfriends.
ANDREI MEDVEDEV, Ukrainian tennis player, 1993

I know it's difficult for you, Lord, we have so many runners.
FATHER SEAN BREEN saying Mass for Irish horses at the Cheltenham Festival, 1993

Any boxer who says he loves boxing is either a liar or a fool. I'm not looking for glory. I'm not looking for titles. I'm not looking for the hall of fame. I'm looking for money. I'm looking for readies.
Boxer CHRIS EUBANK before return match with Nigel Benn, which ended in a draw and thus the possibility of another pay day, 1993

Chess teaches responsibility; if you make a good move you win and a bad move you lose. There's nobody else to blame.
NIGEL SHORT, British Chess Grand Master, 1993

42

Nationalism and National Qualities

England expects this day every man to do his duty.
HORATIO NELSON (1758–1805), British admiral, Battle of
Trafalgar, 1805

It is said, I believe, that to behold the Englishman at his best one
should watch him play tip and run.
RONALD FIRBANK (1886–1926), English novelist, *The Flower
Beneath the Foot*, 1923

Britain believes people of Latin origin have no right to these positions. . . . This is a north–south war, brought about by the superiority
complex of the Anglo-Saxons, who cannot stomach a Spaniard as
head of the IOC [International Olympic Committee].
JUAN ANTONIO SAMARANCH, President of the IOC, 1993

I have this theory that singing the national anthem before the match
dissipates the adrenaline – and I want to keep the lid on my emotions.
I know I will find listening inspiring enough.
NIGEL WALKER, British Olympic hurdler, before first cap for Wales
at rugby union, March 1993

Yes, of course, I supported the changes made by Gorbachev. Most of
us did. I suppose we expected miracles but these have not happened.
Now I must go to the West if I am to remain the best in the world.
SERGUY BUBKA, Ukrainian athlete, on his decision to live in
France, 1991

Talks over Dave Watson's transfer are being hampered by the Bremen
officials' lack of decent English.
PETER SWALES, Chairman of Manchester City FC, 1978

There have been several occasions since he became an England crick-eter when Greig has overplayed his hand. ... What has to be remem-bered of course is that he is not an Englishman by birth or upbringing, but only by adoption. It is not the same thing as being English through and through.
JOHN WOODCOCK, journalist, *The Times*, 1977

Zola Budd will make a great British athlete, her heart lies here.
SIR DAVID ENGLISH, Editor, *Daily Mail*, 1984

In Britain there's a will to win; in America there's a need to win.
GLYNN TIERNAN, *New York Times*, 1988

I feel very hurt that Seles, Sabatini and others can't spare one week in four years to play for their country. I think their attitude is disgrace-ful, especially when they are being offered $500000 in appearance money. It is very sad that they don't seem to have any pride in playing for their country ... such greed could be the germ of the death of the sport.
PHILIPPE CHATRIER, President of the International Tennis
Federation, on the failure of star women to take part in the
Federation Cup in England, June 1991

Australians are aggressive people: they play to win. Historically, we have outfought the odds – from our start as a penal colony. We have been ravaged by nature, through flood and drought, so we know adversity; and we are a nation which chances its arm. That expresses itself in aggression and skill on the field.
ALAN JONES, Australian rugby union coach, 1991

We guts it out better. You have to have that ability ... and I think that's what happened in numerous fields – football, swimming, cricket and golf. Also, I think we want success more. We are so isolated, and it costs so much to travel overseas to compete.
NEALE FRASER, Australian Davis Cup tennis captain, 1991

We are so far away. It's like the country boy coming to the city, with something to prove. So many of our Olympic champions came from nowhere, as complete underdogs.
PHIL COLES, Secretary-General of Australia Olympic Committee,
1991

A bomb under the West car park at Twickenham on an international day would end fascism in England for a generation.
PHILIP TOYNBEE (1916–81), English novelist and journalist

Some people think we have the right to go round the world beating teams comfortably.
GRAHAM TAYLOR, England football manager, 1991

England and America should scrap cricket and baseball and come up with a new game that they can both play; like baseball, for example.
ROBERT BENCHLEY (1889–1945), US humorist and critic

This country's pride is back. We went over and thumped the Iraqis and now we have won this.
PAUL AZINGER, US golfer, on the Ryder Cup, 1991

Having stood on the sidelines for 21 years, I now know how Neil Armstrong felt when he stood on the moon.
CLIVE RICE, South Africa captain, on return to international cricket, v. India, 1991

They think we're just a bunch of ignorant paddies from the bog. Let's not disappoint them.
STEWART McKINNEY, Irish rugby union player, before match with England, 1978

Canada needed that.
Boxer LENNOX LEWIS on winning Olympic title for Canada, 1988

You don't need to be Ironside to know that the man don't live in the country – he's taking the mickey out of the country.
FRANK BRUNO on Lewis (by then a British citizen) before their fight, 1993

The world's a better place when we beat the Australians at cricket.
Former Prime Minister MARGARET THATCHER, 1992

> You love losers, your women are ugly and your men can't fight.
> US boxer JAMES TONEY, IBF super middleweight champion, on the British, 1993

The world's a better place when we beat the Australians at cricket.
Former Prime Minister MARGARET THATCHER, 1992

We did it for Africa, and for African women.
ELANA MEYER, South African athlete, embracing Ethiopia's Derartu Tulu, after Olympic Games, 1992

Britain has football hooligans, Germany has neo-Nazis and France has farmers.
The Times, 1992

As a player, if you are denied the symbols of your country, the flag and the anthem, you are denied your identity – it is just like playing club rugby. It is ridiculous to run onto the field with the Lion lager song.
ULI SCHMIDT, South African rugby union player, 1992

A successful national team is fundamental to promoting interest, from grass roots right to the top. Not just the money for the FA, but the prestige.
ROBERT CHASE, Chairman of Norwich City FC, 1993

Nothing can unite a country like South Africa more than a rugby Test match – we become one.
DANIE CRAVEN, President of South African Rugby Union, 1991

His grandfather once went out with a Polish girl whose uncle once saw Mike Gibson play.
London Irish RFC programme note, explaining the Irish links of new coach Haka Reid (former New Zealand hooker), 1993

It was like being in a foreign country.
IAN RUSH, Welsh footballer, on his unhappy spell playing in Italy, 1992

If I have to choose between betraying my country and betraying my friend, I hope I should have the guts to betray my country.
E. M. FORSTER (1879–1970), English novelist

You can't feel tired when you are playing for your country.
GRAHAM TAYLOR, England football manager, asked about the effect of the long English football season on forthcoming World Cup matches, 1993

We were not fairly beaten, my Lord. No Englishman is ever fairly beaten.
GEORGE BERNARD SHAW (1856–1950), Irish dramatist, in *Saint Joan*, 1923

I'm so patriotic, you know. I love my country. I have been lucky enough to stand there with chest out, chin in, singing the national anthem. That was the ultimate for me.
TERRY BUTCHER, England footballer, 1994

To the Napoleonic charge that England is a nation of shopkeepers it can be replied that it is also a land of football heroes ... when England's claim to footballing greatness unravels, so does its pride.
The Times leader after outcry over England's World Cup defeat by Norway, 5 June 1993

But the truth is that the English are far better at inventing games than at playing them. ... Despondent once again at the failure of its athletes, England should not forget these original sporting heroes who realized that the true national game is not kicking a ball but dreaming new ways of doing so.
The Times leader, 5 June 1993

I was told I could do more for Croatia by playing winning tennis.
GORAN IVANISEVIC, on deciding to stay in tax exile in Monte Carlo, 1992

The whole of the world is tribal, but when it comes to rugby, New Zealand is much more tribal than most. The All Blacks are the national virility symbol. Their people support them come hail, rain or shine.
MIKE GIBSON, former British Lions and Ireland rugby union player, May 1993

Remember that you are an Englishman, and have consequently won first prize in the lottery of life.
CECIL RHODES (1853–1902), South African statesman, quoted in the *Guardian*, 1993

It's our country all over, always worrying about the peripheral things and never the important meat and two veg.
GRAHAM GOOCH, English cricketer, complaining about criticism of England cricket team's dress, 1993

It's good for us to have people who excel at sport; it's good for us to win and we aren't going to win unless we approach it professionally.
Prime Minister JOHN MAJOR, 1993

That's the American flag and I'm an American. But I couldn't salute it in the accepted manner, because it didn't represent me fully; only to the extent of asking me to be great on the running track, then obliging me to come home – be just another nigger.
TOMMIE SMITH, US athlete, reflecting on his Black Power salute at the 200 metre gold medal ceremony, Mexico Olympic Games, 1968

When I run up to the wicket in a Test match I'm bowling to thank England for all they've done for me and my family.
DAVID (SYD) LAWRENCE, English cricketer, 1993

Our decline as a football power started when boot styles changed and the wogs no longer knew what it was like to be on the receiving end of a British toe cap.
MICHAEL PARKINSON, English journalist and broadcaster, 1974

I know I'm not an Ali or a Sugar Ray Leonard. But I have beaten all their records. I do not have a big endorsement. That is because I am a Mexican. But I'm satisfied with what God has given me.
JULIO CESAR CHAVEZ, world light welterweight boxing champion, 1993

Every player loves Wimbledom. Winning is the most coveted honour. The only thing that lets the championship down is the deafening screaming and yelling of the crowd when a Briton – or some great favourite – is on court.
BUNNY AUSTIN, British tennis player, in letter to *The Times*, June 1993

There's a good reason you don't care about soccer ... it's because you are an American, and hating soccer is more American than apple pie, driving a pickup or spending Saturday afternoon channel-surfing with the remote control. ... [For US spectators sport] is all arms and hands, things that happen from the waist up. ... Feet never have been terribly respected in the sports world. ... As somebody who knows what real sports are, you are under no obligation to play footsie with the rest of the world.
TOM WEIR, US columnist, *USA Today*, 1993, looking forward to the staging of the 1994 football World Cup in the USA

I do love cricket – it's so very English.
SARAH BERNHARDT (1844–1923), French actress

If people behaved in the way nations do they would all be put in straitjackets.
TENNESSEE WILLIAMS (1911–83), US playwright

I've had some great chances to see other parts of the world, and I've enjoyed that. But I've never wanted to live anywhere but Britain.
WILL CARLING, England rugby union captain, 1993

The English have no exalted sentiments. They can all be bought.
NAPOLEON BONAPARTE (1769–1821)

You'll never have a quiet world till you knock the patriotism out of the human race.
GEORGE BERNARD SHAW (1856–1950), Irish dramatist, in *O'Flaherty VC*, 1915

When you find some country gentleman keeping up the old English customs at Christmas and so forth, who is he? An American who has just bought the place.
GEORGE BERNARD SHAW

There's a great saying in Ireland, and it's not without irony. It says that the last time we played England we beat them one-all. We so rarely win that anything which gives us a vague reply is seized upon.
JIM SHERIDAN, film director (e.g. *In the Name of the Father*), February 1994

Fifty years from now, Britain will still be the country of long shadows on county grounds, warm beer, invincible green suburbs, dog lovers, and – as George Orwell said – old maids bicycling to holy communion through the morning mist. And, if we get our way, Shakespeare will still be read – even in school. Britain will survive unamendable in all essentials.
Prime Minister JOHN MAJOR, 22 April 1993

Cricket is a game; its purpose is enjoyment, not a form of nationalist propaganda.
JOHN ARLOTT (1914–91), English cricket commentator

43

Olympic Cities

A little mutant monstrosity that was born in the toxic dump of somebody's imagination.
Los Angeles Times on Atlanta's 1996 Olympic mascot, 1992

The Greek Olympic Committee has irrevocably decided not to participate in any events marking celebrations for the 100th anniversary of the revival of the modern Olympic Games.
Statement issued after Athens lost bid for 1996 Centenary Olympic Games to Atlanta, 1990

There is no standard attitude, or general reason for a decision. For some [IOC] members the key point is what's best for the competitors. For others, the concern is to vote with their own bloc – the Latin Americans, for example. There have even been suggestions in the press that some members pledge their votes to the highest bidders – but no one has ever come up with any evidence to back up such claims.
CHARLES PALMER, former Chairman of British Olympic Association, on the methods used to select an Olympic host city, 1992

The Montreal Olympics made money, like their predecessors from 1964 onwards. But all the city projects were lumped onto the Games' balance sheet. It's the redevelopment of Montreal that is still being paid for.
CHARLES PALMER, 1992

The process is nothing more than a lottery. The IOC selection process defies logic, and fortunes have been lost. It's a very costly game to play under the existing rules.
PETER LAWSON, General Secretary of the Central Council of Physical Recreation, 1992

A pitiful spectacle of begging, bribery and intimidation.
The Spectator, 1993, on the IOC Congress at Monte Carlo in
September 1993 which selected Sydney for the 2000 Games

In addition to having a President who is an ex-Fascist, the committee
before which John Major made his undignified and desperate pleas
for Manchester is also made up of a large contingent of unrecon-
structed communists.
The Spectator leader, on the Monte Carlo IOC Congress, 1993

There's only one medal and it lasts for about eight years. It's a fantastic Olympic sport and the most difficult of all.
BOB SCOTT, leader of the Manchester bid for the 2000 Games, on
the Olympic host city bidding process, 1991

The Olympics are the most significant genera-
tor of investment and private equity in the
world today.
ANDREW YOUNG, ex-US Ambassador to
the UN, leader of the successful Atlanta bid
for the 1996 Games; speaking in
Johannesburg, 1993

Eighty per cent watch the Olympics on TV. You can send a message
of hope, of freedom, to the world, through the Games.

We are experiencing the privatization of the Games.

There is nothing that brings new non-government money to a city
like the Olympic Games. ... It is a boost you cannot get from anything else. You cannot lose [bidding for the Games]. The fun is in the
chase. You get to know people in your own community usually you
don't have time to get to know. Sportsmen meet artists, businessmen
meet politicians, etc. The process of bidding pulled us together as a
city like we've never been together before.
ANDREW YOUNG, 1993

The Olympic dream is still ... people of different backgrounds working together.

The Games will take us into the twenty-first century as a major city.

We sold ourselves as an African city, with 67 per cent of the population black; we told the IOC, it's not our fault that we were taken away from there as slaves!
ANDREW YOUNG, 1993

We regard the International Olympic Committee as God.
CHEN XITONG, Secretary of Beijing Communist Party, 1993

We need the 2000 Olympic Games to feed and clothe our people.
CHEN XITONG speaking at IOC Congress at Monte Carlo, September 1993

A more open China awaits the Olympic Games.
Banner in Beijing for the Asian Games, 1993

Those whose entries are regarded as posing a threat to China's national security and social order will not be allowed to enter.
Beijing Olympic bid document to the IOC, 1993

Lack of glamour is our weakness.
BOB SCOTT, leader of Manchester's campaign for the 2000 Games, 1993

Can you trust us? With all our hearts, we say 'yes'. We will present a classic Games at a historic moment. It is 50 years since Britain last had the Games. You trusted us in 1948 when the world was dark; in the bright dawn of a new century, you can trust us.
BOB SCOTT, leader of Manchester bid, in presentation to IOC, 1993

This bid is a unique effort, reflecting unity in British sport ... We are at the heart of the country ... but London will play its part.
CRAIG REEDIE, Chairman of the British Olympic Association in Manchester presentation to IOC, Monte Carlo, 1993

No warmer welcome awaits the athlete. We will stage an athletes' Games and we will break records.
HRH PRINCESS ANNE, in Manchester's presentation to IOC, Monte Carlo, 1993

Ich bin ein Berliner.
President JOHN F. KENNEDY (1917–63), 1962, speech used in Berlin presentation to the Monte Carlo IOC Congress, September 1993

The German Government will do everything to ensure the Games (in Berlin) are as perfect, full of cheer, as can be wished.
MANFRED KANTHER, German Minister for the Interior, at IOC Congress, 1993

There are enough right-wing radicals in Germany who would start talking about a Master race if we won lots of medals in a Berlin Olympics.
BORIS BECKER, German tennis player, opposing Berlin's bid, 1993

The new threat for peace lies at the borders between cultures. Let's not create new walls. ... We are the safest city in Europe, there is a solidarity of cultures in Istanbul.
Prime Minister TANSU ÇILLER of Turkey in Istanbul presentation to IOC, 1993

For the first time in Olympic history, the athletes and officials from all sports will be in one Village. Competitors from 14 sports will be able to walk to their events.

We had earnestness in our presentation. We kept our nerve. The experience of a third campaign helped.
JOHN COATES, President of the Australian Olympic Committee, in presentation for Sydney to IOC, at Monte Carlo, 1993

We went to the brothel every morning to prostitute ourselves and get one more vote for Sydney.
FRANK SARLOR, Sydney's Lord Mayor, about Monte Carlo IOC Congress, 1993

Now there will be lots more depth in Australian sport. Young athletes will see the Games as more reachable and attainable, bringing a resurgence in Aussie sport, every athlete will work that little bit harder.
KIERAN PERKINS, Australian swimmer, at Press Conference after Sydney win, Monte Carlo, 1993

Manchester and Sydney had the same agenda. Both performed well, and reinforced Sydney's position.
KEVIN GOSPER, Australian IOC member, at Press Conference after Sydney's win in Monte Carlo

Sydney should have come last time, they would have beaten Atlanta.
DICK POUND, member of IOC Executive Board, September 1993

The future of the Olympics is in very good hands. We have made the right decision. This was a remarkable bid.
FRANCOIS CERRARD, IOC Director General, at Sydney Press Conference, Monte Carlo, 1993

We did our numbers.
JOHN COATES, President of the Australian Olympic Committee, at Sydney Press Conference, 1993

A good decision for Sydney, for Australia, for the Pacific, for the world, for the Olympic Movement.

A deafening decision, marking out Australia as a nation that can carry the Olympic Games, the world's great event. It shows the world's confidence in Australia – that we can travel on our own, under our own steam.
JOHN KEATING, Premier New South Wales, in Monte Carlo, 1993

The presentations on the final day can move between 5 and 10 per cent of the IOC votes.
KEVIN GOSPER, Australian IOC member, 1993

It was a job. Now, we have a very big obligation to deliver back the investment people made in us.
ROD McGEOCH, Director of Sydney bid, 1993

Final result is expression of contents of Technical Report (by IOC Commission). A very good choice. We are honouring a country, Australia, which has bid three times in a row. A young country, with young people. The Games will not only be great but will set an example for the future.

A lot of politics involved before this vote. But the decision taken by the IOC was really a sports decision. The Games are in very good hands.
JUAN ANTONIO SAMARANCH, President of the IOC, at IOC Press Conference the day after the decision for Sydney, 1993

It is pretty sad to see all this back-biting and petty carry-on. We have not been quite able to handle victory.
PHIL COLES, Australian IOC member, later in 1993

I'm extremely disappointed for those who worked hard but never got a thankyou from anybody and still haven't got a thankyou from anybody, and I think that is very, very disappointing. (But) it is time to prevent any more damage. We have got to get the Games going.
ROD McGEOCH, ex-Director of the Sydney bid, 1993

John, many see you as decent, even reasonably honest as politicians go. But since you have returned from Monte Carlo you've been seen as nothing more or less than a fool.
JOHN VALDER, former President of NSW Liberal Party, and supporter of Sydney bid, in letter to NSW Premier John Keating, leader of presentation team in Monte Carlo

Every change is risky but that's sport. It was a challenge. Now we've modified it. Yet it always comes down to a decision between two in the end.
ANITA DeFRANTZ, US IOC member, after IOC decision to cut down bidding cities to a short list of four, through a special Commission, rather than the two proposed by the Executive Board, 1994

The IOC now believes that, whatever the host city, the income will vary only by a small percentage.
DICK POUND, Chairman of IOC Finance Commission, at Monte Carlo, 1993

It's clear that you don't have to be one of the great countries to host a financially successful Games.
DICK POUND, at Lillehammer, commenting on their success in generating extra income for the Winter Olympic Games, 1994

Olympic Movement

44

Citius, altius, fortius.
Olympic motto

Olympism is not a system. It is a state of mind. It can permeate a wide variety of modes of expression and no single race or era can claim a monopoly of it.
BARON DE COUBERTIN (1863–1937), founder of the modern Olympic Movement

> The most important thing in the Olympic Games is not winning but taking part ... The essential thing in life is not conquering but fighting well.
> BARON DE COUBERTIN, in speech at banquet for officials of London Olympic Games, 24 July 1908

Many similar great spectacles have since then passed before these eyes. Memories of the London stadium have never diminished by comparison. The enormous enclosure, black with people, vibrant with enthusiasm, distilled a sensation of [Olympic] strength that, as far as I am concerned, has never been equalled or inspired by other crowds at home or abroad. The circumstances, in addition, pitted the youth of the Anglo-Saxon [nations] against one another with particular virulence, and gave birth within the Olympic body to a kind of a test of muscular strength between their champions.
BARON DE COUBERTIN recalling changes in the Olympic Games since 1908

The modern Olympic Games symbolize the struggle between man's ideals and the reality within which he must live.
RICHARD ESPY, writer of *The Politics of the Olympic Games*, 1979

The Olympic Games exists for the art of the possible, rather than for ideals. Without such a stance, the Games would never take place at all.
SIMON BARNES, journalist, *The Times*, June 1991

There's a wonderful phrase in Indonesia: 'Where there's sugar, there's ants'. It applies to the whole of the Olympic movement.
CRAIG REEDIE, Chairman of the British Olympic Association, 1992

The Olympics. To me they mean having a friendly time. Having a cup of coffee with the likes of Carl Lewis.
BORIS BECKER, German tennis player, 1992

I think you are living in a strange world when you talk about welcoming in tennis and gold millionaires and basketball players earning $130 million between them and then say there is no room for a sport that is among the few that remains truly amateur.
JIM FOX, British Modern Pentathlete, on suggestions that Modern Pentathlon might be removed from the Games, 1992

For the African it is de rigueur to look after one's family and friends. They have no tradition of Western ethics about gifts, nor of old Victorian principles. They are expected to make the most of their situation. Similarly, I remember serving on committees with colleagues from the Eastern bloc, who simply had no foreign exchange. Their daily expenses would just cover a cup of coffee. Fortunately, now the IOC picks up everyone's daily expenses.
CHARLES PALMER, former Chairman of British Olympic Association, 1992

You may inform them that every penny I have ever had has been earned through my own efforts.
AVERY BRUNDAGE (1887–1975), IOC President, after criticisms from a German magazine about his 'life of ease'

I can see no possible harm that can be done to either golf or to the Games by mutual involvement. Golf has all the right images and behaviour appropriate to the Olympic Games.

There is no threat to amateur status because the players will be competing only for Olympic medals. It seems to me commendable that golf professionals should give up two weeks of money-winning time in order to be part of the Olympic movement.
MICHAEL BONALLACK, Secretary of the Royal and Ancient Golf Club, 1993

The Olympic flag and the flags of the world fly at half mast. Sadly, in this imperfect world, the greater and more important the Games become, the more they are open to commercial, political and now criminal pressure ... We have only the strength of a great ideal. ... The Games must go on and we must continue our efforts to keep them clean, pure and honest and try to extend the sportsmanship of the athletic field into other areas.
AVERY BRUNDAGE, IOC President, at the Memorial Service for those killed by terrorists at the Munich Games, 1972

If you want Olympic Games, don't start wars.
HRH DUKE OF EDINBURGH, 1980

The boycotts are not so terrible. There's no death involved. Olympics have survived massacres, cataclysms, destruction and sixteen centuries of slumber; they are stronger than boycotts.
MONIQUE BERLIOUX, IOC Director, 1984

[The election of the USSR to the IOC, in 1951] was the thin end of a very long wedge. It brought in the state athlete.
CHARLES PALMER, former Chairman of the British Olympic Association, 1992

They are sport's claim to grace. They are the bloodlines, that generate the continuing quality of today's and tomorrow's actors on the stage of sport. The Olympic Games are sport's link with the ancients – even perhaps with the Gods.
COE, TEASDALE, WICKHAM, *More Than a Game*, 1992

45

Opponents

Every time a friend succeeds I die a little.
GORE VIDAL (born 1925), US writer

I no doubt deserved my enemies, but I don't believe I deserved my friends.
WALT WHITMAN (1819–92), US poet

Fuck off Norway.
PAUL GASCOIGNE, English footballer, 1992, before England's World Cup match v. Norway. (It was a joke, for which he later apologized)

To dismiss this lad Denness, you don't have to bowl fast, you just have to run up fast.
BRIAN CLOSE, English cricketer, 1974

I enjoy hitting a batsman more than getting him out. I like to see blood on the pitch. And I've been training on whisky.
JEFF THOMSON, Australian cricketer, 1974

I'll chase the son of a bitch Borg to the ends of the world. I'll be waiting for him. I'll dog him everywhere. Every time he looks round, he'll see my shadow.
JIMMY CONNORS, US tennis player, 1978

He can run, but he can't hide.
US boxer JOE LOUIS (1914–81), on Billy Conn, before title fight, 1946

McCague will go down in Test cricket history as the rat who joined the sinking ship.
Editorial in *Daily Telegraph Mirror* in Sydney, Australia, after Australian trained McCague was picked for England, June 1993

Her tactics are ridiculous. It's annoying and she knows it annoys me but that's to her advantage. One of these days it will be different. I have elbows too, you know.
Athlete LIZ McCOLGAN on race tactics of fellow Scot Yvonne Murray, 1993

Scratch a lover and find a foe.
DOROTHY PARKER (1893–1967), US writer and wit

While the relationship between drivers is superficial, we're the only ones who can talk to each other regarding what we do. We have no one else to relate to.
PETER REVSON (1939–74), US motor racing driver, 1973

Never ascribe to an opponent motives meaner than your own.
J. M. BARRIE (1860–1937), Scottish writer, 1922

I'd like this team to grow in humility and not to treat victory as a means of putting another human being down. I take great exception to people who scorn the opposition.
ALAN DAVIES, Welsh rugby union team coach, 1994

Always forgive your enemies – but never forget their names.
ROBERT F. KENNEDY (1925–1968), when US Attorney General

46

Performance

England needs the commitment of a Coe or Ovett in its team games. The cricketers have it too easy. The leadership is too soft; the preparation isn't hard enough. In Australia, we train as hard in outdoor sports as Coe and Ovett did on the track.
ALAN JONES, Australian rugby union coach, 1991

Only think of two things – the gun and the tape. When you hear the one, just run like hell until you break the other.
SAM MUSSABINI, athletics coach (to Harold Abrahams, amongst others)

When you win the toss, bat. If you are in doubt about it, think – then bat. If you have very big doubts, consult a colleague – then bat.
W. G. GRACE (1848–1915), English cricketer

The greatest professional quality is not money, but attitude.
JOHN MONIE, Australian rugby league coach working in Britain, 1993

I've seen people freeze. When it's full, it's an intimidating sight. Before a player bowls, the din is deafening. In the moment before delivery a deadly hush descends. If the ball hits the pad, there is pandemonium.
KEITH FLETCHER, England cricket manager, about Eden Gardens, Calcutta, before first Test v. India, 1993

I do want to play the long ball and I do want to play the short ball. I think long and short balls is what football is all about.
BOBBY ROBSON, England football manager, c. 1986

I am a firm believer that if you score one goal the other team have to score two to win.
HOWARD WILKINSON, Leeds United FC manager, 1992

Speed? Really the whole process is the reverse of speed, how to eliminate it. It doesn't exist for me, except when I am driving poorly. The things seem to be coming at me quickly instead of passing in slow motion and I know I'm off form.
JACKIE STEWART, world motor racing champion, 1972

I am able to get to a level where I am ahead of myself: maybe a fifth of a second, who knows? When my car goes into a corner, I am already at the apex.
AYRTON SENNA (1960–94), Brazilian motor racing driver, 1991

It doesn't matter how quick you are, you can't play rugby without a brain.
DAVID CAMPESE, Australian rugby union player, on tour in France, October 1993

I may not have been very tall. I may not have been very athletic. But the one thing I did have was the most effective backside in world rugby.
JIM GLENNON, Irish rugby player, 1991

To give you an idea of how fast we travelled – we left with two rabbits, and when we arrived we still had only two.
BOB HOPE, US entertainer

A good darts player who can count can always beat a brilliant one who can't.
LEIGHTON REES, Welsh darts player, 1977

I just want to get out in the middle and get the right sort of runs.
English cricketer ROBIN SMITH, suffering from stomach virus on India tour, 1993

England's cricketers have thoroughly enjoyed their week in Portugal. But, as preparation for the Caribbean, arguably the toughest tour of the lot, it is the equivalent of walking the dog prior to running the London Marathon.
VIC MARKS, ex-England cricketer, journalist, commenting on England's week in Portugal preparing for the tour of the West Indies, December 1993

If the Patron can score a goal, of course you pass to him.
ADUARDO HEGUYS on the niceties of being a polo professional in a millionaire's amateur team in England, 1993

The fellows in the executive boxes [at Everton] are the lucky ones. They can draw the curtains.
STAN BOARDMAN, British comedian, 1993

The race is not actually taking place.
Aintree public address system, after false starts to the Grand National, March 1993

He couldn't start a race for white mice.
DAVID NICHOLSON, racehorse trainer, on Aintree starter, March 1993

I died out there. It was an absolute nightmare.
CAPTAIN KEN BROWN, Aintree starter, March 1993

My leotard got twisted and stuck right up my bottom just as I was getting to the hurdle. Bit of an unwanted distraction, really.
SALLY GUNNELL, British athlete, after World Championships semi-finals, 1993; she then won the title and broke the world record

The only thing that scares me is the Americans' dress sense.
Golfer MARK JAMES before Ryder Cup, 1993

> People say you're only as good as your last game, so we're not very good are we?
> GRAHAM TAYLOR, England football manager, before match v. Poland which England won, September 1993

His day will come another night.
BOBBY ROBSON, England football manager, on Ray Wilkins, after 2–1 defeat by Republic of Ireland, 1985

Hump it, bump it, whack it. It might be a recipe for a good sex life but it won't win the World Cup.
KEN BATES, Chairman of Chelsea FC, on England's World Cup performances, 1993

It's no good fucking crying – I've got no sympathy. Don't cry on me.
CHRISTOPHER DEAN to JAYNE TORVILL, British ice dancers during practise for their comeback to the Winter Olympics, March 1994

We were playing a role – in love for just two minutes (Torvill). Now we're just good friends again (Dean).
TORVILL AND DEAN, after comeback January 1994

If what Torvill and Dean do on ice is deemed merely middlebrow showbusiness, sport could do with more of it. ... If other sports gave markes for artistic impression, David Gower would still be batting, Henri Leconte would always win Wimbledon, Severiano Ballesteros would win championships more often than he does, and Jeremy Guscott would be shimmying through the midfield for all eternity. And the sporting firmament would be brighter.
The Times leader, 10 January 1994

47

Politics

If Stalin had learned to play cricket the world might now be a better place to live in.
DR R. DOWNEY (1881–1953), Archbishop of Liverpool

Men trifle with their business and their politics; but never trifle with their games. It brings truth home to them. They cannot pretend that they have won when they have lost, nor that they have made a magnificent drive when they have foozled it. The Englishman is at his best on the links, and at his worst in the Cabinet.
GEORGE BERNARD SHAW (1856–1950), Irish dramatist

I know more about football than politics.
Former Prime Minister HAROLD WILSON, 1973

The politics involved make me nostalgic for the Middle East.
HENRY KISSINGER, US statesman, after FIFA rejected the USA bid he led to stage the World Cup, 1983

It is quieter, less controversial, more reflective and more physical [than sport].
British athlete SEBASTIAN COE on politics, 1989

Sport and politics are ever blood brothers.
SIMON BARNES, journalist, *The Times*, 1991

I ain't got no quarrel with the Viet Cong.
MUHAMMAD ALI, US boxer, *c.* 1965

Being in politics is like being a football coach. You have to be smart enough to understand the game and dumb enough to think it's important.
EUGENE McCARTHY, US politician, 1989

Whoever said sport had nothing to do with politics made a very great mistake.
JUAN ANTONIO SAMARANCH, President of the International Olympic Committee, 1992

Michael Jordan has already mastered the skill most needed for political success: how to stay aloft without visible means of support.
Former Prime Minister MARGARET THATCHER, 1992

Sport and chivalrous competition awakens the best human qualities ... it helps to strengthen the bonds of peace between the nations. May the Olympic flame therefore never be extinguished.
ADOLF HITLER (1889–1945), German Chancellor, 1935

All the laws regulating the Olympic Games shall be observed. As a principle, German Jews shall not be excluded from German teams at the Games.
Written guarantee secured by IOC before Berlin Games, 1936

A glance at the hierarchy of the British Olympic Association shows how aristocratic the direction of the athletics was in Britain at that date.
DUFF HART-DAVIS, Writer of *Hitler's Olympics*, 1986

The British Olympic Council are convinced that in sending a team to Berlin they are acting in the best interests of sport.
Council's letter to *The Times*, March 1935

The Americans should be ashamed of themselves, letting negroes win their medals for them. I shall not shake hands with this negro.
ADOLF HITLER, as recorded by von Schirach, Reich Youth leader, as Jesse Owens mounted rostrum, Berlin Olympic Games, 1936

The miners' strike is ridiculous. There's tea ladies at the top of a mine who are earning more than county cricketers. Arthur Scargill ought to come down here and try bowling 20 overs.
RAY ILLINGWORTH, English cricketer, c. 1974

Sir: So, the Home Secretary has no power to ban this foreign director coming here to make a film showing Jesus in the nude, drinking and lovemaking. Yet no such problem arose when the Government wanted to ban a Rhodesian cricket team.
Letter in the *Daily Telegraph*, 1976

If only politicians had to sweat it out to get to the Olympics, they might not be so keen to say to we sportspeople, 'Sorry, you're not going'.
HRH PRINCESS ANNE, 1975

I am not going to be a standard-bearer for people on either side of the debate. In the end, this is a decision that must come from inside every individual not from outside pressure.
SEBASTIAN COE, British athlete, on the Moscow Olympic Games boycott issue, 1980

There are infinitely more important things in life than the Olympics, such as being loyal to one's country. I don't think the Russians should be allowed to get away with invading other people's countries. It's just not on, frankly.
LUCINDA PRIOR-PALMER (later Green), British equestrienne, on the same issue, 1980

It seems to us ironic that politicians are always quick to cash in on sporting success but not so quick to lend financial support.
ARTHUR McALLISTER, British athletics chairman, 1987

What we want is for you to get your hooligans out of our game.
TED CROKER, FA General Secretary, to Prime Minister Margaret Thatcher at Downing Street meeting on football hooliganism, 1985

Is there anyone running this game? Is there someone we could speak to?
Prime Minister MARGARET THATCHER, to her civil servants, 1985

There are more hooligans in the House of Commons than at a football match.
BRIAN CLOUGH, football manager, 1980

Were cricket and football abolished, it would bring upon the masses nothing but misery, depression, sloth, indiscipline and disorder.
LORD BIRKENHEAD (1872–1930), Attorney General, 1911

East Germany cultivates a sporting conception of the state, and a state conception of sport.
JEAN MARIE BROHM, French gymnastics coach, 1978

The West Indies exists on the cricket field, and in the minds of men, just as a united Ireland exists on the rugby field. ... Cricket plays a central role in West Indian society. Its body of laws, as well as the tacit codes that go with it, have helped to define the attitude of citizens to public order and social responsibility. ... These factors have helped to protect democracy, even in difficult times. ... The game is not, of course, a panacea. But its absence does impoverish society.
The Times leader, 17 January 1994

It is international sport that helps kick the world downhill. Started by foolish athletes, who thought it would promote understanding, it is supported today by the desire for political prestige and by the interests involved in gate money. It is completely harmful.
E. M. FORSTER (1879–1970), English novelist, 1957

When I toured South Africa with Oxbridge Jazzhats, I became physically ill after a week. We were being used for propaganda. I will never return there.
DEREK PRINGLE, English cricketer, 1982

Multiracial sport, or isolation. That seems the logical choice for South Africa.
CARWYN JAMES, British Lions rugby union coach, 1974

It is political commitment and political belief that can make a man think that his opponent's views are so obnoxious that he will abstain from playing any game with him as a protest against what the other man believes in. ... Any man's political commitment, if it is deep enough, is his personal philosophy, and it governs his way of life, it governs his belief, and it governs the people with whom he is prepared to mix.
JOHN ARLOTT (1914–91), cricket commentator, in debate at
Cambridge Union, 1970

To persist with the tour seems to me a social, political and cricketing error. ... There are three justifiable reasons for playing cricket – performance, pleasure and profit – and I do not believe that this tour will produce any of them.
JOHN ARLOTT, on South African cricket tour of UK, 1970

I had black friends as a boy, but we used to get separated when we went to events like soccer matches. ... In 1961 blacks were suddenly banned from even watching white teams play. But some were so keen they shinned up trees overlooking the Caledonian stadium. I recall the screams as police with dogs hauled them down; they were taken away, bleeding and with clothes torn. All to preserve the sanctity of an all-white sporting occasion.

PETER HAIN, MP and leading activist against 1970 South African cricket tour of UK, reflecting in 1992 on his childhood in Pretoria, South Africa

I never thought the MCC would take a decision on moral or political grounds. The MCC didn't have a moral view about South Africa. They ran cricket according to cricket's needs and had no wider or moral principles. The only way to make an impact was by direct action.

PETER HAIN, MP on the MCC's decision over the 1970 summer tour, 1992

One of the crosses radical protestors have to bear is that they are not popular at the time. But I was never in the business of striking poses. The objective was to get a non-racial system in South Africa. Even people like Danie Craven eventually admitted that our campaign was justified.

PETER HAIN, 1992

We are like a train standing at the station. We cannot wait if people do not get on.
JEAN-CLAUDE GANGA, IOC member for Congo, on the readmission of South Africa to the Olympic Games, June 1991

If we give the Springbok away, what will be left for us whites?
DANIE CRAVEN, President of South African Rugby Union, 1976

The mental violence caused by apartheid has wrought far more anguish and suffering than any bombs planted by the ANC. Just think of the grief caused to black people by their exclusion from so many spheres of South African life. You cannot blame people so discriminated against for taking action. It is we – the whites – who have caused the violence.
DANIE CRAVEN, 1989

Rugby led the way in attacking this Government and in becoming an autonomous body. The other sports eventually jumped on the bandwagon.
DANIE CRAVEN, 1990

It's not our intention to deprive people of rugby but we don't think rugby should be a celebration of white supremacy.
Spokesman for African National Congress (ANC), 1992

42 000 people are saying they recognize the need for peace in our country. I feel more confident than ever that the country will be saved. That moment of silence saved South Africa.
STEVE TSHWETE, ANC, on minute's silence at South Africa v. Australia rugby Test match for victims of apartheid violence, 1992

We were crucial to the National Party's strategy. Had we not been here, or if things had gone badly for us, they would probably still have won, but I don't think it would have been so convincing. So our involvement in Australia [in the cricket World Cup] had an effect.
KEPLER WESSELS, South Africa captain, after his country's referendum, March 1992

It was the final abolition of most of the apartheid laws which motivated the international community and sports movement to reconsider their attitude towards South African sport. [The boycott] . . .

was undoubtedly responsible for highlighting the issue of apartheid internationally.
SAM RAMSAMY, formerly head of SANROC, Chairman of National Olympic Committee of South Africa (NOCSA), speaking in 1992

The people in the country most optimistic about South Africa are those going for the Olympics. They are confident about the changes, they are not afraid of them, and therefore they will go forward and achieve them.
ANDREW YOUNG, ex-US Ambassador to the UN and leader of the successful Atlanta Olympic bid, Johannesburg, March 1993

We are free people playing an amateur game [rugby] and we have got the right to play where we like ... as sure as hell we can play our game in South Africa.
DENNIS THATCHER, husband of British Prime Minister Margaret Thatcher, December 1979

British athletes have the same rights and the same responsibilities towards freedom and its maintenance as every citizen of the UK ... for British athletes to take part in the Games in Moscow ... would be for them to seem to condone an international crime.
Prime Minister MARGARET THATCHER, in letter to British Olympic Association, February 1980

First, we considered this was a decision for sport. But if the Government had said to us, 'look, we have decided not to trade any more with the USSR because of this issue of principle', then we'd have felt we were part of a unified, consistent national policy. But we couldn't avoid the feeling that sport was being picked off as a cheap option.
PETER LAWSON, General Secretary of the Central Council of Physical Recreation, 1992, about the Moscow Olympic boycott 1980

The Department is about what people do when they're not working. What they do with the rest of their lives. That is a thread which runs through all those things ...
PETER BROOKE, Secretary of State for National Heritage (which includes sport), April 1993

Peter Brooke – a man who doesn't know his arts from his elbow.
WILLIAM WHYTE, Labour spokesman, Party Conference, 1993

For the last twelve years I've been manager there's been practically a civil war in Northern Ireland and yet my teams have been a mixture of both tribes, who roomed together, worked together, played together. Isn't it amazing? If the rest [of society] could reflect that, there wouldn't be much trouble in Northern Ireland.
BILLY BINGHAM, Northern Ireland football manager, 1993

You will never get me to say I regret that [trip to South Africa on a rebel tour]. I did what I did because cricketers should be allowed to earn a living anywhere that English businessmen are allowed to. Why were only sportsmen pilloried?
GRAHAM GOOCH, English cricketer, on 1982 South Africa Breweries tour, September 1993

There are no true friendships in politics. We are all sharks circling, waiting for traces of blood to appear in the water.
ALAN CLARK, former Conservative Minister, Summer 1993

Sport is a way out of war, as well as a way into it.
The Times leader, 21 March, 1994, reflecting on sport in war after football match in Sarajevo between a youthful local side and the UN Protection Force

Please stop the fighting, please stop the killing, please drop your guns.
IOC President JUAN ANTONIO SAMARANCH, opening Winter Olympic Games at Lillehammer, 12 February 1994, in plea to combatants at 1984 Winter Olympic city of Sarajevo (and before one minute silence)

Politicians are like nappies. Both should be changed regularly and for the same reason. Happy Xmas and 1994.
Graffiti in Yeovil, December 1993

48

Race

Baseball is very big with my people. It figures. It's the only time we can get to shake a bat at a white man without starting a riot.
DICK GREGORY, *From the Back of the Bus*, 1962

To fight in South Africa would be an affront to my family, my country and my integrity.
JOHN CONTEH, British boxer, 1974

Whites seem to enjoy seeing black boxers broke. Rolls Royce are broke. Nixon's broke. What's their excuse? But people still say, 'ain't it terrible that Joe Louis is broke?'

I began the poetry and predicting rounds. And it worked. They started coming with their ten and twenty dollar bills to see the bragging nigger. ... How do I know who the greatest fighter was?
MUHAMMAD ALI, US boxer, 1973

There was a great deal of fuss about being the first black Junior Davis Cup player, the first black to win a tennis scholarship to UCLA ... the fact that this kind of accomplishment by a black player got so much attention was an indication that we still had so far to go.

Growing up black was harder than having AIDS.
ARTHUR ASHE (1943–93), US tennis player, *c.* 1990

After sweatin' in fields all day as I did, I'm not goin' to stand for all that Uncle Tom crap.
JOE FRAZIER, US boxer, 1971

There is no apartheid practised in South Africa's Grand Prix because there are no coloured drivers or spectators.
MIKE REID, English comedian and actor, 1982

It remains to be seen whether blacks have what it takes to adapt to the rigours of tennis. We are always hearing how good they are at sprinting and jumping, but apart from Ashe and Althea Gibson, there hasn't been one who has risen to the top. Maybe it has something to do with nature.
PHILIPPE CHATRIER, President of the International Tennis Federation, 1982

The main social disease in the US is race; in Britain, historically at least, it is class. Both countries like to see the record of black athletes as evidence of an increasingly tolerant society. But observe the double whammy; the fall of Johnson and Tyson are used, at least implicitly, to show how far black people still have to go before they reach white standards.
SIMON BARNES, journalist, *The Times,* February 1992

I don't care if he's black or white or yellow with purple spots, if he can do a job for West Bromwich Albion he's in the team.
RON ATKINSON, English football manager about 'The Three Degrees' – Batson, Moses and Regis – in his West Bromwich Albion football team, 1972

Kill the nigger.
Constant shout from fight 'fans' at Clay v. Liston title fight, 1964

You have to speak eight languages just to set the field.
GRAHAM GOOCH, on England's multiracial cricket team, 1991

This morning our practice was England v. the All Sorts, and the All Sorts won 4–1. Sometimes it's the black kids v. the white kids. I have no problem with race or colour.
RON ATKINSON, football manager, 1993

When you get into deep midwinter in England, you need a few of the hard white men to carry the artistic black men.
RON NOADES, Chairman of Crystal Palace Football Club, 1991

We are sort of show horses out there for the white people. They give us peanuts, pat us on the back say, 'Boy, you did us fine'.
JOHN CARLOS, US athlete, after his Black Power salute with Tommie Smith after the 200 metres at the Mexico City Olympic Games, 1968

I came back to my native country and I could not ride in the front of the bus. .... I was not invited to shake hands with Hitler, but I was not invited to the White House to shake hands with the President either.
JESSE OWENS (1913–80), US athlete, after winning four gold medals at the Berlin Games, 1936

Neither Owens nor any black champion was pictured in the *Atlanta Constitution*, the most liberal of southern newspapers.
PROFESSOR A. GUTTMAN, *The Games Must Go On*, 1984

Humanity is more important than winning a gold medal. What I pray for is not a gold medal but equality.
FILBERT BAYI, Tanzanian athlete

My memory of the summer of 1960 is not the hero's welcome, the celebrations ... the Mayor, the Governor ... but that night I stood on the Jefferson County Bridge and threw my Olympic gold medal down to the bottom of the Ohio River.
CASSIUS CLAY (later Muhammad Ali), US boxer

If I could give you one gift, it would be a life free of racial discrimination.
ARTHUR ASHE (1943–93), US tennis player, in letter to his daughter Camera, published after his death, 1993

There's no apartheid now. Any killings out there are black against black.
ALAN WHICKER, broadcaster, on South Africa, September 1993

White folks would have forgiven the black socks, the silk scarf, the bowed head. But they saw that raised black fist and were afraid.
TOMMIE SMITH, US athlete, 1993, 25 years after he and John Carlos gave the Black Power salute at the 200 metre medal ceremony at the Mexico Olympics

The single most courageous act of the century.
MUHAMMAD ALI, US boxer, on the Smith/Carlos Black Power salute in 1968

I was afraid, deathly afraid. Every little crack I heard I thought I was a goner ... we were wide open out there. We'd been threatened hundreds of times. .... The 1960s were a real sorry time.
TOMMIE SMITH, 1993

49

Records

The four minute mile was a matter of shadow rather than substance.
A piece of good fortune ... nothing more.
SIR ROGER BANNISTER, British athlete, ex-Chairman of the
Sports Council, April 1994

When they complain about my attitude, I'd like them to explain how I
compiled my Test record.
DAVID GOWER, English cricketer, 1992

I was pleased with the throw but it wasn't perfect technically. I've
watched it on the video and I think the next competition can be better.
JAN ZELEZNY, Czech athlete, after setting new world javelin
record of 95.45 m, at Pietersburg, South Africa, April 1993

If Jan had a telegraph pole in his hand on Tuesday it would have gone
90 metres.
TOM PETRANOFF, South African javelin champion, same day

It's a great milestone but it was hanging there and it's good to get it
out of the way so that I can now concentrate on batting. I wanted to do
it in Australia and especially here in Sydney.

I might have a few more runs left in me yet. The Gavaskar figure is
now the goal and I'll try to set something up for someone else to try
and get past.
ALLAN BORDER, Australian cricket captain, on becoming second
player to pass 10 000 runs in Test cricket, 3 January 1993

When I lost my world record I took it like a man. I only cried for ten
hours.
DALEY THOMPSON, British athlete, 1980

I cannot break it, it is so far.
HUANG ZHIHONG, Chinese world champion woman shotputter,
discussing the world record putt of 22.63 metres set by Natalya
Lisovskaya of the old USSR in 1987; October 1993

Cricket is notoriously a little more than a game and a little less than a
religion. It is the only activity in which the present can be ranked
against the past so precisely. Nobody compares modern novelists and
their scores by the age of 23 with Dickens, or politicians with Pitt.
Cricket, because of its antiquity and complexity, and having *Wisden*
... and other tablets of stone to record the ancient scores, is the best
game for number crunchers. ... Graham Thorpe's debutant century,
besides alleviating the nation's grumpiness, has written him a foot-
note to the kind of record that lasts longer in England than the annals
of budgets and royal commissions.
The Times leader, after drawn third test against Australia in which
Thorpe scored a century in his first Test match, July 1993

50

Referees and Umpires

You cannot be serious . . .
JOHN McENROE, US tennis player

How can you put a £5 referee in charge of a £20 000 competition?
ALUN EVANS, Cardiff coach, after 16–14 defeat in Welsh Cup by junior club, St Peter's, January 1993

The road to being a top referee is littered with broken marriages.

If at the end of the game, the losing team thinks you are quite a good bloke, you've probably done a good job.
ROGER QUITTENTON, English rugby union referee, 1992

The secret of being a good umpire is to do as many matches as possible which inevitably puts a strain on your professional life. You need an accommodating employer.

Everyone makes errors. The difference between the best umpires and the linesmen is that they make fewer.
JOHN RELPH, British Tennis Umpires Association, February 1992

I feel two teams are like two chemicals and the referee is the catalyst. If you get a good reaction, you get a good product.
NEIL MIDGELEY, FIFA referee, 1992

The missus is the ultimate Mrs Rothschild. For the full ninety minutes every Saturday she spends as I earn. She regularly travels with me but has actually watched only five football matches in her life. Instead she can lead you blindfold into every Marks & Spencer from Torquay to Tyneside.
ROGER MILFORD, FA Cup Final referee, 1991

The court said it was strange for a husband to complain about his wife spending too much time on football.
WENDY TOMS, English referee, on the break-up of her marriage, 1992

The referee said he was a friend of mine and it was his duty to see I did not leave the field in that way.
SERGE BLANCO, French rugby union player, on his punch in the France v. England match, World Cup, 1991

When a referee is in doubt, I think he is justified in deciding against the side that makes the most noise.
A. H. ALMOND, referee, after awarding Scotland a try in the first rugby union international, Scotland v. England, 1871

There is a refereeing reflex which always counts against the French. This separates the reputedly noble adult nations from a sort of Third World of rugby. The French team, no doubt, has been relegated to this subclass.
DENNIS LALANNE, French sportswriter, 1992

It's a disgrace to suggest referees take charge of the French with any preconceived ideas.
FRED HOWARD, English international rugby union referee, 1992

I have always had sympathy for French referees. Their rugby is quite violent. You need to be an absolute headcase to be a referee out there.
CLIVE NORLING, Welsh international rugby union referee, 1992

I have no argument with the French dismissals, but referees have to work for uniformity.
PIERRE BERBIZIER, French rugby union coach, 1992, after match v. England in which two French players were sent off

Mike Ditka regrets about 99 per cent of the naughty things he does, but he still thinks he was right to spit on a referee this year.
Washington Post profile of Ditka, legendary coach of Chicago Bears, 1988

> The trouble with referees is that they just don't care which side wins.
> TOM CANTERBURY, US basketball player, 1980

Us managers have a problem with referees now because their mistakes affect our livelihood and a lot of the players. The referee can get out his car, go home and he's not responsible to anyone but it's our livelihood ... we must do something about it. The League Managers' Association, together with the Press, must act. Come on, you lot got Kinnock out!
BOBBY GOULD, Coventry City FC manager, in comments to Press after 1–1 draw at Norwich, January 1993

I don't need managers coming up to me saying, 'You've lost us the game and that could cost me my job'. Managers can't keep blaming referees if their side doesn't win.
ALF BUKSH, retiring as a Football League referee, 1993

The umpire admitted to me afterwards that he'd given me out lbw to Jim Parks because he was desperate for a pee.
DENIS COMPTON, English cricketer, reflecting on batting at number eleven in his first championship match for Middlesex (in 1936), 1993

If I can't ask a linesman about a bit of pushing, then we've got no chance.
GRAEME SOUNESS, Liverpool FC manager, after being ordered from the pitchside at Crystal Palace, 1993

They were continually arguing about the way Mr Hopkins was refereeing the game. To have this kind of soccer terraces attitude brought to a school rugby match is just not on.
PETER JACKSON, head of Highfield School, Hertfordshire, banning two fathers after they had forced the abandonment of an Under 13s match against the Knights Templar School, 1993

Tell the referee he's just cost me my job, will you?
GRAHAM TAYLOR, England football manager, to linesman at
World Cup match v. Holland, October 1993

Did you win a lottery to be linesman?
JOHN McENROE, US tennis player, on a disputed call, 1991

Refereeing is a balance between tolerance and neo-fascism – I tend to
lean towards the latter.
DAVID ELLERAY, English football referee (including the 1994 FA
Cup Final), 1994

Players and spectators at all levels can enjoy sport better if they totally
accept two simple rules:
Rule 1: The referee is always right.
Rule 2: In the event of the referee being obviously wrong, Rule 1
applies.
PETER CORRIGAN, journalist, 1994

51

Resignation (and Sacking)

I resigned as coach because of illness and fatigue. The fans were sick and tired of me.
JOHN RALSTON, Denver Broncos football team, 1978

The decision had to be made. It should've been made ten years ago.
FRED TRUEMAN, English cricketer, on the decision to sack Geoffrey Boycott, 1983

I don't know of another club in history which finished bottom of the league, sacked its star player and left the manager in the job. The Yorkshire Committee are guilty of the biggest whitewash I can recall.
BRIAN CLOUGH, football manager, 1983

Sport has a high wastage rate, like turtles and the sea.
STEVE COPPELL, English football manager, *c.* 1990

I may one day leave Liverpool, but Liverpool will never leave me.
KENNY DALGLISH, footballer and football manager, 1989

It wasn't a change of heart. I have to hold my hands up and admit I bottled it. It was a very emotive day for me when I went up to Sheffield to tell them I was leaving and I should have gone through with the decision there and then. If the news hadn't leaked, I would have done.

I've been racing Formula One in a Mini Metro.
BOBBY GOULD explaining his resignation as manager of Coventry City FC, 1993

It's been arguably the biggest decision I've ever had to make in football. I can understand that the Sheffield people may feel that I have let them down ... and I have to admit that I probably have.
RON ATKINSON, football manager, June 1991, after announcing that after all he was leaving Sheffield Wednesday for Aston Villa; having announced only a week before that he would stay

There's not a cat in hell's chance that I'm going to walk out. It's not in my nature to walk away from things. That's something that has to be decided by other people.
GRAEME SOUNESS, Liverpool FC manager, 1993

There was a lot of pressure on me to stay. They told me there was no reason for me to go, that it wasn't my fault ... I told them things weren't happening for me. Players just weren't responding; they wanted to, but somehow I couldn't get it out of them. It was time for a change.
GRAHAM GOOCH on his resignation from the England cricket captaincy, 1993

52

Retirement

Retirement is the ugliest word in the language.
ERNEST HEMINGWAY (1899–1961), US novelist

To retire is the beginning of death.
PABLO CASALS (1876–1973), Spanish cellist

Eating's going to be a whole new ball game. I may even have to buy a new pair of trousers.
LESTER PIGGOTT, English jockey, on his (first) retirement, 1991

Few men of action have been able to make a graceful retirement at the right time.
MALCOLM MUGGERIDGE (1903–90), British journalist and broadcaster

I can tell you now that I'll know exactly when I want to retire; but when I reach that time I may not know.
JACK NICKLAUS, US golfer, 1977

Jackie Stewart faces two options, neither of them very appealing. He can quit racing and save his life, or he can quit racing and lose what his life is about.
FRANCOIS CEVERT, French motor racing driver, the day before he died, 1973

When a man retires and time is no longer a matter of urgent importance, his colleagues generally present him with a watch.
R. C. SHERRIFF (1896–1975), English playwright and novelist

I will not play soccer professionally again. For the time being it's an irrevocable decision.
DIEGO MARADONA, Argentinian footballer, 1991

Of course, I will miss the game. There is simply no substitute for the buzz which international rugby brings. But more than the hype, the most satisfying element is that each time it lays down a unique challenge; the opportunity to test yourself against the best in a hostile physical environment. That test, which has now gone on for ever, will be the most difficult facet of my life to replace and is the reason why some sportsmen carry on longer than they ought. It is difficult voluntarily to deny the one area of your life in which you excel.

And now, I can't get used to the hair gel and body lotions after the game!
PAUL ACKFORD, England rugby union forward, on his retirement, 1991

I have seriously thought about retiring, but that was on a good day. On a bad day I've thought about killing myself.
IVAN LENDL, US tennis player, after once again failing to win Wimbledon, 1992

I'm looking forward to it very much. I think it beats the hell out of life after death, that's for sure.
MARTINA NAVRATILOVA, US tennis player, on life after tennis, July 1993

I don't want to kill myself struggling for seventh place.
JAMES HUNT (1947–93), English motor racing driver, on his retirement

The word 'retire' means you can do anything you want, maybe that's the challenge I'll need some time down the road. I'm not going to close the door.
MICHAEL JORDAN, US basketball player, 1993

Sportsmen often hang in there because they feel they do not have a better alternative, even though they are past their prime.
IMRAN KHAN, Pakistan cricket captain, September 1993

I've achieved everything I could, from an individual standpoint and a team standpoint. That's what made it easy to walk away.
MICHAEL JORDAN announcing his retirement, September 1993

Old big 'ead has just had enough.
BRIAN CLOUGH, football manager, May 1993

You've wined and dined on me for a long time, but you're not going to
see me around anymore.
BRIAN CLOUGH, May 1993

It's the end of that era really, with Bill Shankly, Bob Paisley and Don
Revie. It's the end of the old-fashioned figureheads at clubs who ruled
everything that happened there.
TERRY YORATH, Wales football manager, on Brian Clough's
retirement, 1993

It's a very hard decision to make, but there were times last season
when I thought: 'What am I doing here?'
Cricketer DAVID GOWER announcing his retirement after failing to
be selected again for England, 1993

When you are in sport you are tied into it. . . . It takes a strange person
to give up. It's a much more natural process to try and fight. I don't
think it's a clever thing to retire at the top. I'm sure Bjorn Borg
regrets it. I think it's best to go out screaming.
STEVE DAVIS, British snooker player, 1994

53

Royalty

It's all to do with the training; you can do a lot if you're properly trained.
HM THE QUEEN, 1992

Oh, do turn it off, it is so embarrassing unless one is there – like hearing the Lord's Prayer when playing Canasta.
QUEEN ELIZABETH THE QUEEN MOTHER, when the National Anthem was being played at a televised Cup Final

If you find you are to be presented to The Queen, do not rush up to her. She will eventually be brought round to you, like a dessert trolley at a good restaurant.
Advice in *Los Angeles Times*, 1983

She isn't a bad bit of goods, The Queen! I wish all the fleas in my bed were as good.
MIGUEL DE CERVANTES (1547–1616), Spanish novelist, in *Don Quixote*, 1605

In the midst stood Prince Henry, who showed already something of royalty in his demeanour, in which there was a certain dignity combined with singular courtesy.
ERASMUS (1466–1536), Dutch scholar, on first meeting the future Henry VIII

I'm tired of carrying the can for all of them. I've been the scapegoat of the Waleses for the past four years.
THE DUCHESS OF YORK, 1993

Well, she was wearing dark glasses, wasn't she?
Ascot race course gateman, after turning away the Princess Royal, 1993

54

Seasons, Times and Weather

It is very nearly too hot for Europeans to play cricket.
KEITH FLETCHER, England cricket manager, in India, 1993

It's a funny kind of month, October. For the really keen cricket fan, it's when you discover that your wife left you in May.
DENNIS NORDEN, British television presenter, *She*, 1977

I don't mind the fight going out at 3 o'clock in the morning. Everyone in Glasgow fights at 3 in the morning.
JIM WATT, Scottish boxer, 1980

If I can see 'em, I can hit 'em.
DAVID HUGHES, Lancashire cricketer, at 9.00 p.m. in fading light before scoring 24 runs in an over to win a Gillette Cup semi-final, 1971

Spring is the season of balls – golf, tennis, base and moth.
L. L. LEVINSON, US lexicographer

The only thing I didn't understand about the English is why they're so interested in the weather. One day it's light grey, the next day it's dark grey.
ERIC CANTONA, French footballer, 1992

People ask me if I had trouble sleeping and I never did. It was waking up that was the problem.
TERRY VENABLES, football manager, after leaving Tottenham Hotspur, September 1993

What dreadful hot weather we have! It keeps me in a continual state of inelegance.
JANE AUSTEN (1775–1817), English novelist, letter, 18 September 1796

As time requireth, a man of marvellous mirth and pastimes, and sometimes of as sad gravity, as who say: a man for all seasons.
ROBERT WHITTINGTON, English sixteenth-century writer, about Sir Thomas More

If Watford could put the game back ten years, it would be in a better state than it is now. There would be no £1 million players and wages to suit, there would be less debts, and more fans would be watching.
DANNY BLANCHFLOWER (1926–93), Tottenham Hotspur and Northern Ireland captain, as a *Sunday Express* journalist, responding to Terry Venables' criticisms that Watford (under Graham Taylor's management) had set the English game back ten years

Selection and Selectors

I didn't play Gascoigne because I always pick the foreigners according to their physical condition.
DINO ZOFF, Lazio manager, 1993

I've reached that awkward age for any sportsman – too old physically to carry on competing at the top level, but still too mentally alert to become a selector.
SEBASTIAN COE, British athlete, 1990

We're going there to win and you can't do that if you compromise on selection.

Going on tour can destroy some people with its emotional pressures, so, in selection, you are looking at character as well as ability.
IAN McGEECHAN, British Lions rugby union coach, 1993

This marvellous game of ours has been hijacked by one or two people. The selectors are either incompetent, inert, inept, or all three.
DENNIS OLIVER, leader of campaign against England cricket selectors over India tour 1992/93; at MCC debate, Central Hall, Westminster, January 1993

Try telling Montgomery he could not select the side he wanted. I have nothing but the highest praise for the England captain – even if he does wish to have players he is comfortable with.
LORD BRAMALL, MCC member, speaking against the motion, January 1993

I don't approve of these rebellions. But I've read what you have to say. Thought it was better than the other side. So I'm abstaining.
UNNAMED PEER, in discussion with newspaper editor Donald Trelford, before MCC vote

I don't drop players. I make changes.
BILL SHANKLY (1913–81), football manager, 1973

We prefer not to use the word 'dropped'. Mullin has just been left out.
KEN REID, Ireland rugby union manager, *c.* 1988

I haven't seen the lad, but my coaches have and he also comes hugely recommended by my greengrocer.
BRIAN CLOUGH, football manager, on signing Nigel Jemson, 1988

It is horrible when you are not in the team ... you wonder what is going to happen. There is a lot of uncertainty. Everyone wants to play. They say you get good money, but you are doing it for yourself, for your pride.
JAMIE REDKNAPP, English footballer, 1993

I didn't want to be waving to my home crowd from the back of the field.
British athlete KRISS AKABUSI withdrawing from a farewell appearance at Crystal Palace when Andy Norman signed up Olympic champion Kevin Young to run in the race, 1993

56

Sponsorship

Is not a Patron, my Lord, one who looks with unconcern on a man struggling for life in the water, and when he has reached the ground, encumbers him with help?
DR SAMUEL JOHNSON (1709–84), English lexicographer, in letter to Lord Chesterfield, 1755

We are by far the most powerful influence on sport in the world. We could turn any individual sport – golf, tennis, skiing – on its ear tomorrow.
MARK McCORMACK, International Management Group (IMG), chairman and founder, 1975

They should call it the International Management Group Invitation, not the World Matchplay Championship.
Spanish golfer JOSE-MARIA OLAZABAL on his non-invitation to the tournament by IMG, when rated world number two, because he was not on IMG's books

It is most undesirable that an organisation should be able to represent a governing body, sponsors, a significant number of top players, negotiate television, cable and satellite contracts, and sell merchandising rights. The situation is pregnant with conflicts of interest and cannot carry public confidence.
1983 Report of the Committee of Inquiry into Sports Sponsorship, chaired by Denis Howell, MP

If you took 100 of these stories about our being ruthless or sharklike, ninety of them would centre on attitudes we have taken on behalf of our clients. I think being ruthless, in the context in which it is applied to me, is really sort of a compliment.
MARK McCORMACK, IMG, 1992

I still maintain it's very unfair to have agents owning tournaments and it's easy for them to persuade players to play.

Money is the biggest problem we face in tennis.

Our game is really in danger of dying from too much money. You cannot blame a brilliant young player who takes, say, £120 000 ($210 000), which he or she is offered to play for just one night. But it gives them a totally false impression of life and what their tennis priorities ought to be.
PHILIPPE CHATRIER, President of the International Tennis Federation, *c.* 1990

If I were the directors of Admiral I'd be looking for a get-out clause in the clothing contract before the England team did our product any more damage.
MICHAEL PARKINSON, English journalist and broadcaster, 1976

BBC cameras picked up a solemn lady called Paula Fudge as she pounded along a running track with BRITISH MEAT written across her understandably heaving bosom. Sponsorship in sport is one thing, but this was altogether a different kettle of offal.
DENNIS POTTER (1935–94), English playwright, 1978

My son bought a new cricket ball. On it in gold lettering it said: 'Gunn & Moore Ltd, Nottingham' with 'England' added for good measure. Underneath in tiny letters, not in gold, hardly visible at all, the words 'Made in India' are stamped.
ALAN WATKINS, English cricketer, 1975

And Atherton's looking pretty comfortable out there ... and if you want to be comfortable when you're visiting the North west, why not stay at the Mottram Hotel in Cheshire ...?
BOB WILLIS, England cricketer and broadcaster, commentating on Lancashire's Benson & Hedges match v. Kent at Old Trafford on Sky TV, 1992

Canon League? Some teams are so negative they could be sponsored by Kodak.
TOMMY DOCHERTY, football manager, 1983

John Player are getting cut price exposure for a company banned by law from directly advertising its products on TV.
IAN WOOLDRIDGE, English journalist, 1971

I don't believe anybody will start smoking simply because a tobacco manufacturer has sponsored a race or rally.
PETER COOPER, Royal Automobile Club Chief Executive, 1980

I'd like to thank Embassy but unfortunately I don't smoke.
STEVE DAVIS on winning World Snooker Championship, 1981

Tobacco sponsorship enables the companies to associate cigarettes with healthy, glamorous and life enhancing activities ... and above all enables [them] to get round the ban on cigarette advertising on TV. Tobacco sponsorship is designed to change the public perception of cigarettes and the companies who deal with them.
PETER TAYLOR, *The Smoke Ring – Tobacco, Money and International Politics*, 1984

If the British Government wants to move people off smoking then they should make it illegal. ... Sport is struggling for support; without sponsorship, sport would wither.
PETER LAWSON, General Secretary of the Central Council of Physical Recreation, *c.* 1986

People ask for anything with André's name on it.
DICK DILLON, Donnay's US sales director, on the appeal of
Agassi, 1991

Grand Prix racing is a commercial break at 150 mph.
PETER DUNN, British journalist, 1991

The days of deals being decided on the whim of the chairman are
gone.
IAN MUIR, Chairman of Institute of Sports Sponsorship, 1992

Coca Cola can use its status as a main sponsor of the Games to pro-
claim, mystifyingly, that it is 'sharing the Olympic ideal'. What sporting ideal, exactly, can a soft drink share?
RICHARD WITHAM, journalist, *Independent*, 1992

In some quarters there are those, it seems, who think that the future
belongs not to the spin bowler but to the man who paints logos on the
outfield.
GRAEME WRIGHT, editorial in *Wisden*, 1992

Test match sponsorship has lifted our company from the top end of
the middle of the insurance company league into the first division.
Thanks directly to this sponsorship, the only item in our promotional
budget, we are now as well known as the other major insurance companies. It's good value for money.
JEFF MAYHEW, Cornhill Insurance, on his company's Test cricket
sponsorship, 1992

Sport is something which everyone can relate to: everyone has been
involved in sport at some time or another.

Each [sponsorship] has a purpose. Polo brought us exactly the image
we wanted at the time. Darts, on the other hand, gave us the audience
buying our product; motor and rallying gave us development opportunities for product, and football ties us immediately into the local
community.
PATRICK FITZ-GIBBON, Unipart Ltd, 1992

Eighty per cent of Tyrrell Racing's costs are covered by sponsorship. If you don't get results, you can't get or even keep your sponsors. If you don't get the sponsorship, you can't invest. If you don't invest, you can't compete.
BOB TYRRELL, Managing Director, Tyrrell Racing, 1992

[Puma] believes that Becker's Wimbledon victories generated sales of $50 million.
NEIL WILSON, *The Sports Business: The Men and The Money*, 1988

Sandown Park, and all supporters of chasing, have a great deal to thank Colonel Whitbread and his firm for the magnificent prize money they are offering for the Whitbread Gold Cup Chase.
Sporting Life, on the occasion of the first serious sponsorship in British sport, 1957

Value for money! You bet. There is no other promotional area on which we can get such a bang for the buck.
LEO MEHL, Goodyear racing manager, quoted in Coe, Teasdale, Wickham, *More Than a Game*, 1992

Ivan Lendl, the six million dollar man; from head to foot, from sunglasses to tennis shoes, the world champion is estimated to be worth $6 million (£3.7 million) in endorsements by various companies – three times his winnings last year. Some £2.5 million of that figure is derived from exhibitions and public appearances. Game, set and cash to Lendl!
The *Independent* newspaper, 1991

To bring finance into the sport you need sponsors – they are good people to have around but they want something out if they put something in. However, the future of all sports is in their hands; as they all depend heavily on sponsorship these days.
GRAHAM GOOCH, English cricketer, 1994

The bottom line is that the endorsement has to help you sell more units of product. But you also use this to help create an image in the market, or to establish brand identification and loyalty.
SEBASTIAN COE, British athlete, as Chairman of Diadora (UK), 1992

The ideal [person package] is a winner who can speak well, especially if they can speak a few languages. ... somebody who can present themselves well, and can speak well of the product.
CHRIS HANNA, Salomon (ski equipment) sales director for North America, 1992

Nostalgia has a place in the game but we are in changing times.
FRAN COTTON, of Cotton Traders, defending another change in England rugby union kit, 1992

57

Style

In matters of grave importance, style, not sincerity, is the vital thing.
OSCAR WILDE (1854–1900), Irish wit and playwright, in *The Importance of Being Earnest*, 1895

Man, I sure like your style, but I like my height better.
CORNELIUS JOHNSON, US high jumper, at 1936 Berlin Olympic Games, watching the different technique of Britain's Arthur Gold

In his century at Headingley, Boycott touched the ankle of his right foot 40 times each hour. He took off his cap and wiped his brow 364 times. He played 466 balls. He marks his guard twice every time he gets down to the business end, one at the usual mark, the other inside his crease.
JACK FINGLETON, Australian cricketer and journalist, 1977

There goes a woman who knows all the things that can be taught and none of the things that cannot be taught.
COCO CHANEL (1883–1971), French dress designer

They are kicking the ball 50 yards instead of 60.
MIKE WALKER, Norwich City manager, when asked if Wimbledon had changed their style of football in 1993/4 season, 1993

I do not play cricket, as it obliges me to assume such indecent positions.
OSCAR WILDE (1854–1900), Irish wit and playwright

Life is a game. The idiosyncrasy of the English is that they pretend that cricket is also a game. ... All sport, especially cricket, is an irrational activity, and part of its pleasure is disagreeing with the selectors and imagining that one could do better oneself.
The Times leader before MCC EGM on a vote of no confidence in the England cricket selectors (over the 'David Gower affair'), 1993

58

Talent and Genius

Every man of genius is considerably helped by being dead.
ROBERT LYND (1879–1949), Anglo-Irish essayist/journalist

Doing easily what others find difficult is talent; doing what is impossible for talent is genius.
HENRI AMIEL (1821–81), Swiss philosopher/poet

Whom the Gods wish to destroy they first call promising.
CYRIL CONNOLLY (1903–74), British critic

Man can climb to the highest summits but he cannot dwell there long.
GEORGE BERNARD SHAW (1856–1950), Irish dramatist, in
Candida

Some are born great, some achieve greatness, and some have greatness thrust upon them.
Malvolio in SHAKESPEARE, *Twelfth Night*, 1601

I pay no attention whatever to anyone's praise or blame. I simply follow my own feelings.
WOLFGANG AMADEUS MOZART (1756–91), Austrian composer,
in letter to his father, 1781

To be great is to be misunderstood.
R. W. EMERSON (1803–82), US poet/essayist/philosopher

A man can do no better than beat the best around in his time.
C. B. FRY (1872–1956), English footballer, cricketer and athlete

You should never give the first kick but the adversary has to realize the second will be yours. In my career I got hit a lot, but I also left a lot of people by the wayside.
PELE, Brazilian footballer, on violence in soccer, 1982

Gower is in a different class. His bat is such an extension of his arms and wrists that the blade often apears to be flexible.
H. F. ELLIS, English writer, 1978

In cricket it separated Bradman and Sobers from the rest; Pele had it in football, Borg had it in tennis, Ali had it in boxing, Barry John had it in rugby. Those who try to pin down everything in life like so many butterflies to a board would call it genius. I prefer it nameless.
GEORGE ALLEN, US sportswriter

The weight of Jack Hobbs' run scoring is of historic importance; but it misses the essence of his cricket. He had all the gifts of a great batsman. No one else . . . ever batted with more consummate skill than his, which was based essentially on an infallible sympathy with the bowled ball. Although he could improvise with quite impish virtuosity, it is no exaggeration to say that frequently, even generally, the spectator felt that the stroke he played seemed so natural as to be inevitable.
JOHN ARLOTT (1914–91), cricket commentator, 1981

I have never known a really great athlete (Zatopek, Kuts, Bannister, Elliott, Clarke, Ovett, Coe) who did not have abundant courage and intelligence.
CHRIS BRASHER, British athlete and journalist, 1992

Genius is great when it is on song. It is more of a nuisance when it goes bad, because it contaminates and destroys what is around it.
JOE MERCER, English footballer and manager (including of the England team)

Paul is more precious than the Crown jewels.
IAN WRIGHT, Arsenal and England footballer, on Paul Gascoigne, 1993

He may be an awkward character on the circuit, but only God could have given him that talent – I mean that. In a racing car, he's Superman.
FRANK WILLIAMS, Grand Prix team-owner, on Nigel Mansell, 1992

McEnroe was a genius, cast from the same mould as George Best, Barry John and Viv Richards. They all had an uncanny facility for creating the illusion, mainly by instinct, of having more time and space in which to operate than anyone else.
DAVID IRVINE, journalist, *Guardian*, 1992

You don't just become great. The more you work, within reason, the better you become. And the older you are, the harder you have to practise.
KEITH FLETCHER, England cricket manager, 1992

Good and bad, it is Gascoigne. He does things that make you ask yourself the question, 'Magnificent, but how did he manage it?' Then there are times when you scream, 'Why?' He can make love with a football or he can frustrate you . . . If you work with a genius, you have to accept things differently and try to adapt – as he has to.
DINO ZOFF, Lazio manager, May 1993

Since when was genius found respectable?
ELIZABETH BARRETT BROWNING (1806–61), English poet, in *Aurora Leigh*, 1857

Woolley was never mechanically consistent. His uncertainty was that of an April day and it was entirely natural – was bred and matured in a period which called cricket . . . a game of 'glorious uncertainty'.

His first appearance in county cricket was at Old Trafford in June 1906. He was this day born fully fledged; he never improved on the ease and grace of this baptismal innings. It could not be improved on. His cricket was spontaneously and miraculously created. And miracles are not subject to development.
NEVILLE CARDUS (1889–1975), English music critic and cricket writer, the *Guardian*, on the occasion of Frank Woolley's birthday, 27 May 1967

His driving is unbelievable. I don't go that far on my holidays.
IAN BAKER-FINCH, Australian golfer, on US golfer John Daly, 1992

A reunion of the Beatles could be as poignant as the sight of Bjorn Borg trying to take on younger and fitter opponents with his old wooden racket.
The Times leader, December 1992, on the possible re-grouping of the Beatles.

Stewardess: 'Mr Ali, please fasten your seat belt'.
Mohammad Ali: 'Superman don't need no seat belt'.
Stewardess: 'Superman don't need no plane either'.
Sports Illustrated, 1980

We're just very grateful he's here. He's such a great player. I'm still pinching myself. A player like that only comes along once or twice in a lifetime, and you don't leave him out or put him in the reserves. You respect his skill. Eric is the brainiest player I've seen, he sees such a lot when he has the ball, and this team is perfectly suited to him.
BOBBY CHARLTON, English footballer, director of Manchester
United FC, on Eric Cantona, December 1993

Eric likes to do what he likes when he likes because he likes it – and then f..k off. We'd all want a bit of that.
HOWARD WILKINSON, Leeds United FC manager, on Eric
Cantona, earlier in 1993

The finest, the most honourable defender I ever played against. Moore was my friend.
PELE, Brazilian footballer; on Bobby Moore, captain of England, at his death, 1993.

God must have had a big game coming up.
Wreath at Upton Park, West Ham United's ground, after Moore's
funeral, 1993

Botham lacked caution, prudence, meanness; he was extrovert, generous, courageous, a bit grandiose. He had never had to learn the hard way, and was unable to do so in the second half of his career.
MIKE BREARLEY, English cricketer and captain, 1993

Potential is a word that means you aren't worth a damn yet.
JEFF VAN NOTE, American footballer

Talent develops in quiet places, character in the full current of human life.
JOHANN WOLFGANG VON GOETHE (1749–1832), German poet,
dramatist and scientist

A career is born in public – talent in privacy.
MARILYN MONROE (1926–62), US actress

59

Team Spirit

The bird a nest,
The spider a web,
Man friendship.
WILLIAM BLAKE (1757–1827), English poet and artist

Rather the bite of a friend than the kiss of an enemy.
SHALOM ALEICHEM (1859–1916), Russian novelist

Grief can take care of itself, but to get the full value of a joy you must have somebody to divide it with.
MARK TWAIN (1835–1910), US writer and wit

The differences between friends cannot but reinforce their friendship.
MAO TSE-TUNG (1893–1976), Chinese statesman

The only thing to do is to hug one's friends tight and to do one's job.
EDITH WHARTON (1862–1937), US writer

Anybody can sympathize with the sufferings of a friend, but it requires a very fine nature to sympathize with a friend's success.
OSCAR WILDE

Please accept my resignation. I don't want to belong to any club that will accept me as a member.
GROUCHO MARX (1890–1977), US humorist

Both sides did the right thing and went in to help their mates. That's what I would expect from my side.
BRAD MEURANT, North Harbour coach, after brawl in rugby union match v. British Lions, May 1993

The team just needs time together, and not so much to be coached as to practise together. If golfers don't get back to the practice ground, they quickly slide, just like a musician. There would be a domestic improvement, internationally, if our players had fewer matches.
STEVE COPPELL, football manager, on the England team, 1993

The team spirit inherent in all international sport gives scope to a number of truly valuable patterns of social behaviour which are essentially motivated by aggression, and which, in all probability, have evolved under the selection pressure of tribal warfare at the very dawn of culture.
KONRAD LORENZ (1903–89), Austrian zoologist, *On Aggression*, 1966

You son, you could start a riot in a graveyard.
Liverpool FC manager BILL SHANKLY (1913–81), to his captain Tommy Smith

It's the collective part of the team which is important. If I'd wanted to draw attention to myself I'd have played singles tennis, or chosen a nice lady for mixed doubles.
ERIC CANTONA, French footballer, as Manchester United went top of the FA Premier League, 1993

> It is the closest you'll get to going to war. You are playing a very physical game and you look after each other – if someone is on the floor being kicked, you go in there, you get down to basics, you get close to each other, you have respect for someone who is taking it alongside you.
> WILL CARLING, England rugby union captain, October 1993

I'd much rather have that fellow inside my tent pissing out, than outside my tent pissing in.
US President LYNDON JOHNSON, talking about FBI boss J. Edgar Hoover

We are so tied together that we are almost like a brand name.
CHRISTOPHER DEAN of Torvill and Dean, British ice dancers, 1993

Some days we can spend the whole day arguing. ... (Torvill) But it's only to do with skating the step (Dean).
TORVILL AND DEAN, December 1993, preparing for their Winter Olympic comeback in 1994

Where do you think most of this poison is coming from? The dispossessed and the never possessed. You can think of ex-Ministers going around causing lots of trouble. We don't want another three more of the bastards out there.
Prime Minister JOHN MAJOR, in a recorded but unguarded moment with ITV's Michael Brunson after a TV interview following a series of close votes in the House of Commons on the Maastricht Treaty, 1993

60

Technology

Men have become the tools of their tools.
H. D. THOREAU (1817–62), US writer

I don't want to sound paranoid, but that machine knows who I am.
JOHN McENROE, US tennis player, on the Cyclops electronic line judge, US Open, 1989

Psychologically, it has transformed me completely. There is no doubt that it has definitely improved my game. I feel much more sure of myself and on the field that brings a sort of composure and inner strength that had been lacking before.
DIDIER CAMBARABERO, January 1993, French rugby union player, on his hairpiece, first installed 1988

All a successful downhiller needs is good skis, good boots and no brains.
PAUL ACCOLA, slalom skier, 1991

The automobile changed our dress, manners, social customs, vacation habits, the shape of our cities, consumer purchasing patterns, common tastes and positions in intercourse.
JOHN KEATS, *The Insolent Chariots*, 1958

What is good for the country is good for General Motors, and what is good for General Motors is good for the country.
CHARLES E. WILSON (1890–1961), President of General Motors

The wheel that squeaks the loudest is the one that gets the grease.
JOSH BILLINGS (1818–85), American humorist

What is called the World Drivers' Championship is in fact the Car Manufacturers' Championship. Drivers are becoming irrelevant these days.
JAMES HUNT (1947–93), English motor racing driver, 1979

The computer said the car would work with narrow wheel rims but the bloody computer wasn't strapped in the driving seat.
FRED GARDNER, test driver, after driving the new Porsche 917, 1970

Funding a Grand Prix team is being in the risk business.
FRANK WILLIAMS, Grand Prix team-owner, 1992

[Grand Prix racing] is an artistic form of bear baiting, in which the beast has to be teased and coaxed and teased some more, but never so much that it can bite back, because it bites back bad.
JOHN WATSON, motor racing driver, 1981

I want to be challenged, by my own limits together with someone else's limits, by someone who is made of the same skin and bone, and where the difference is between brain and experience and adaptation to the course; not challenged by someone else's computer.
AYRTON SENNA (1960–94) Brazilian motor racing driver, 1993

In 1988/89, we still had to figure out the problem [as drivers]. Now the difference between the [computerized] cars is huge.
AYRTON SENNA (1960–94), Brazilian motor racing driver, 1993

If I was banned from using glues in this tournament, I wouldn't have a chance.
JAN-OVE WALDNER, Swedish table tennis Olympic champion, on the need to reglue bats twice a day or more in order to remain competitive, 1993

Javelin throwing could turn into a competition between the manufacturers rather than the throwers.
JOHN RODDA, English journalist, the *Guardian*, 1991

If there was only one recognized javelin, if anyone threw it further it would always be on their own merit, not on rival manufacturers' technological improvements.
STEVE BACKLEY, British world record javelin thrower, 1991

Formula One has more in common with the aerospace industry than with the motor car industry.
BOB TYRRELL, Managing Director, Tyrrell Racing, 1991

Not only is there no God, but try getting a plumber at weekends.
WOODY ALLEN, US humorist and film director

Any sufficiently advanced technology is indistinguishable from magic.
ARTHUR C. CLARKE, US author, in *The Lost Worlds of 2001*, 1971

61

Violence

Boxing's just showbusiness with blood.
FRANK BRUNO, British boxer, 1991

Boxing is not morally defensible. If it were banned, it would just go underground. The demand is so strong. It is dangerous – that's what people come to see. Surely, it's better to have it out in the open and then exercise the right and proper controls?
COLIN HART, British journalist, c. 1990

One can reach a point of humiliation where violence is the only outlet.
ARTHUR KOESTLER (1905–83), British author

We boil at different degrees.
R. W. EMERSON (1803–82), US poet/essayist/philosopher

Violence suits those who have nothing to lose.
JEAN-PAUL SARTRE (1905–80), French philosopher

No, I never broke my nose playing ice hockey; but eleven other guys did.
GORDIE HOWE, Canadian ice-hockey player, 1981

Cynical, dirty bastards. A lot of shirt pulling, offside, sneaky boots and punches. We sorted it out. We gave them a good rucking and the punches stopped.
PAUL BURNELL, Scotland rugby union player, after losing 9–15 to France, 1991

My fist was in an unfortunate collision with the head of Queensland forward, Sam Scott-Young.
English rugby union player WADE DOOLEY after breaking his hand during England tour match, 1991

I remember playing against Richard Loe of New Zealand in the World Cup. He'd booted me in the ear in a Barbarians game, so I gave him a dig. He started to come back at me, but then he suddenly saw Wade [Dooley] standing there smiling at him. That was the end of it, but there he was, letting it go. Teaches you something, doesn't it? You can always get found out.
JASON LEONARD, English rugby union player, 1994

If you're going over the top on me you've got to put me out of the game because I'll be coming back for you, whether it's in the next 5 minutes or next season.
VINNY JONES, Wimbledon footballer, 1992

Vinny is a hero of the masses. He represents the bulldog spirit of England. He's never set out to maim anyone.
SAM HAMMAM, Chairman of Wimbledon FC, 1992

He wouldn't have lasted 5 minutes in my day.
TOMMY SMITH, ex-Liverpool and England footballer, on Vinny Jones, 1992

It's tough on the lad but that's the sign of a good centre half. All the best ones have broken noses and cut eyes.
IAN BRANFOOT, Southampton manager, on Richard Hall, 1992

I will do my best but Rome was not built in a day.
RICHARD ASTRE, new French rugby union manager, on instilling discipline in French team, 1992

We're here to play rugby not to get our heads kicked in.
Australian prop DAN CROWLEY after suffering head injury v. Munster, 1992

An arm came up between my legs from behind and grabbed the only assets I have.
SAM SCOTT-YOUNG of Australia after rugby union tour match v. Neath, 1992

We enjoy going to the big clubs and poking them in the eye. We love putting their faces out of joint.
JOE KINNEAR, Wimbledon FC manager; these remarks in December 1993 caused a furore because one of his players (John Fashanu) had been involved recently in an incident with Gary Mabbutt of Spurs in which the latter had suffered serious facial injuries

This tour was a great showcase for the game, but how many mothers will now be saying, 'I don't want my son to play rugby?'
WILL CARLING, England captain, after All Black tour in which he and others criticized them for dirty play, Autumn 1993

The game's always been physical. There was probably just as much violence before but now there's more linesmen, television and video evidence whereas fifty years ago the game was just something to enjoy and read about in the papers. It has got faster and men have got bigger and stronger but percentage-wise it's still very good value, without that many problems. It's the nature of the game to have aggression. Take on people physically and then have a beer with your friends.
GARETH CHILCOTT, Bath and England player, on violence in modern rugby union, 1993

Violence has increased over the past few years. With the prizes so much greater and the obsession with leagues, the philosophy is to win at all costs. More people now bend the rules. Governing bodies are failing to punish offenders adequately and we are setting a terrible example to the younger generation. The rule of law in sport is as essential as the rule of law in society. Without the rule of law in society, you have anarchy; without the rule of law in sport, you have chaos.
EDWARD GRAYSON, barrister, author of *Sport and the Law* (1971), 1993

The rules of the sport should primarily govern the behaviour of the player, not the law of the land. In an ideal world there is no place for sport in the courts.
NIGEL HOOK, Central Council for Physical Recreation, 1993

> If he was in a good mood, he'd put iodine on his studs.
> JIMMY GREAVES, English footballer and commentator, reflecting on Chelsea player Ron 'Chopper' Harris

It's a man's game and men make tackles and I hope men accept tackles without bleating too much.
STEVE COPPELL, football manager, 1990

Pro football is like nuclear warfare. There are no winners, only survivors.
FRANK GIFFORD, *Sports Illustrated*, 1960

Hard men are nothing new in football. In my young days there were quite a few killers about, men who went in for rough play and intimidation. But you wouldn't expect one team to have more than a couple of them. What is new and frightening about the present situation is that you have entire sides that have physical hardness as their main asset.
SIR MATT BUSBY (1909–94), British footballer and manager of Manchester United FC, 1969

Soccer may not have become more violent but it is becoming more cynical. We live in the age of the professional foul, and it doesn't take long for that cynicism to pass down to humbler levels. Fair play is no longer a theme of Britain and that is echoed in sport. We don't live in a fair society, so why should sport be fair?

I spent most of my youth watching third–division soccer. Centre forwards used to shoulder charge goalkeepers into the net, and centre halves and full backs were pretty much killers in their tackling – there were a lot of broken legs.
DENNIS BRAILSFORD, author of *British Sport: A Social History* (1992), December 1993

Wherein is nothing but beastly fury and extreme violence, whereof proceedeth hurt; and consequently rancour and malice do remain with them that be wounded.
SIR THOMAS ELYOT (?1490–1546), English diplomat, referring to football

I don't know if I'd be so keen to play Test cricket these days if I thought I was no more than a physical and verbal target.
SIR COLIN COWDREY, English cricketer and administrator, 1993

Our gallant fellows at the front are carrying their football training into practice on the battlefield. They are 'playing the game' in all conscience.
LORD BADEN-POWELL (1857–1941), founder of Boy Scouts movement, in *Headquarters Gazette*, 1914

Polo today is a game for maniacs. It's controlled warfare.
BRYAN MORRISON, co-owner Royal Berkshire Polo Club, 1993

Cricket is a gentle pastime. Baseball is war!
ALBERT SPALDING (1850–1915), US baseball player and businessman

I went to a fight last night and an ice hockey game broke out.
RODNEY DANGERFIELD, comedian, 1978

Most sorts of diversion in men, children and other animals are an imitation of fighting.
JONATHAN SWIFT (1667–1745), Irish satirist, *Thoughts on Various Subjects,* 1711

We take nothing from no one and give it out to everybody, always. Football is war.
SAM HAMMAM, Chairman of Wimbledon FC, 1993

Why don't we just kill her?
We don't need to kill her. Why don't we just hit her on the knee?
Voices on tape revealing a plot to cripple US ice-skater Nancy Kerrigan, 1993

62

Winning

Winning isn't everything. It's the only thing.
VINCE LOMBARDI (1913–70), American football coach

When in doubt, win the trick.
EDMUND DOYLE (1672–1769), English writer on cards

You may have to fight a battle more than once to win it.
Prime Minister MARGARET THATCHER, 1980

Your first win is like making love and you enjoy it so much the first time that you want to do it again and again.
NIGEL MANSELL on winning the South Africa Grand Prix soon after his British victory, 1985

That is the whole secret of successful fighting. Get your enemy at a disadvantage; and never, on any account, fight him on equal terms.
GEORGE BERNARD SHAW (1856–1950), Irish dramatist, in *Arms and the Man*, 1898

Winning is a drug. Once you have experienced it, you cannot do without it. You live for it.
BERNARD HUNT, British golfer, 1973

Win any way you can, as long as you can get away with it.
LEO DUROCHER (born 1906), Brooklyn Dodgers manager

The pleasure of playing games comes from the small vanity of beating our opponents.
C. NESTELL BOVEE (1820–1904), American writer

It signifies nothing to play well and lose.
THOMAS FULLER (1654–1734), English physician

Winning can be defined as the science of being totally prepared.
GEORGE ALLEN, US sportswriter

Win as if you were used to it, lose as if you liked it.
ANON

The public like to see winners lose.
BILLIE JEAN KING, US tennis player, 1980

Winners aren't popular. Losers often are.
VIRGINIA WADE, English tennis player, 1982

Winning or not winning a world championship is not so important. It is only a transient moment in life.
AYRTON SENNA (1960–94), Brazilian motor racing driver, 1989

The more I win the more I want it. I am dependent upon it.
AYRTON SENNA, 1994

Win the last point.
JIM COURIER, US tennis player, when asked for the key to the French final before the match, 1991

Neither success nor failure is ever final.
Motto of RON DENNIS, owner of McLaren Grand Prix racing team

You can't play sport hoping not to lose; you've got to play with an unapologetic commitment to win.
ALAN JONES, Australian rugby union coach, *c*. 1990

Chess is ruthless; you've got to be prepared to kill people.
NIGEL SHORT, British Chess Grand Master, 1993

Success comes slowly; it doesn't come instantly. And if you work hard enough and you're honest about your deeds, and you've got the talent, then you'll get to the top.
JOHN WALKER, New Zealand athlete

I'm a winner, people find that stern. That is what I have to be. Once I get in the ring, I will do what I have to do to win.
CHRIS EUBANK, British boxer, November 1991

Do you ever get bored by caviar?
MARTINA NAVRATILOVA, US tennis player, on her desire to win Wimbledon again, 1991

The only thing I regret is that I had no time to smell the roses.
IAN BAKER-FINCH, Australian golfer, on winning the British Open golf, 1991

I'm just an emotional little petal.
NICK FALDO, British golfer, after winning the British Open the following year

Well, for one thing, I find I no longer win every golf game I play.
GEORGE BUSH on what it is like not to be President of the USA, January 1994

I like to win. I despise that in myself but it's all there is.
PAUL NEWMAN, US actor, on car racing, 1993

If the chance to run comes along ... I will try to take it, but I don't think people in Ireland are too worried about style – the emphasis on winning is enormous.
NIALL MALONE before his first cap as Ireland's rugby union fly half, 1993

If you want to win you have got to work for it. ... Cricket is now a very physically demanding game. Of course it's very technical too, but I haven't seen anybody who has made themselves fitter and stronger and made themselves a worse player. If you are unfit, you get tired quicker.
GRAHAM GOOCH, English cricketer, April 1993

The other pairs were racing for the silver medal. We had done the work months before in training and in beating them time and again, showing our strength in different areas. They knew they would lose. I love thinking about the final. It was an awesome feeling. In rowing, leading is wonderful because you can watch what's happening behind you. For three minutes we had the best seat to watch the final, and the winner of the race we watched won the silver medal.
MATTHEW PINSENT, GB Olympic rowing gold medallist (with Steven Redgrave), reflecting on the Barcelona final, 1992

Winning is simply concentration, application and confidence.
BRENDON FOSTER, British athlete and commentator, 1974

When you win, nothing hurts.
JOE NAMATH, American footballer

At squash there is a fantastic and savage and unrivalled and unbelievable satisfaction at the moment you know you have beaten your opponent. There is simply no feeling on earth like it – it is a primitive thing, a conquest, an utter victory. You look into his eyes and you see the defeat there, the degradation, the humiliation, the beaten look and there isn't anything in the world like it.
JONAH BARRINGTON, former world squash champion, 1992

I enjoy acquiring the skills of motor racing. It's exhilarating, but nowhere as exhilarating as athletics used to be. I guess athletics mattered a lot more, and what I liked most was winning.
DALEY THOMPSON, British athlete, 1993

I don't deserve this award – but I have arthritis and I don't deserve that either.
JACK BENNY (1894–1974), US comedian

If you live long enough, you'll see that every victory turns into a defeat.
SIMONE DE BEAUVOIR (1908–86), French novelist and feminist

> To be at the top of my sport, you have to have that killer instinct and, when I'm at the table, I'm an animal.
> STEVEN HENDRY after beating Jimmy White in World Snooker Final, 1993

If it takes a world record to win, Sally will run a world record.
BRUCE LONGDEN, Sally Gunnell's coach, the day before she won the 400 metre world hurdles title in a world record time, 1993

Look here, I'm afraid being tryless is always totally irrelevant. The object of rugby is just to score more points than the opposition. End of story.
GEOFF COOKE, England rugby union manager, commenting on England's run of a year and five matches without scoring a try, and after win over France in Paris, March 1994

I always said I might cry if I won but never if I lost.
LILLIAN BOARD, British athlete, 1968

63

The Worst Job in the World?

[It's] living in a goldfish bowl.
GEOFF COOKE, England rugby union manager, announcing his
plans to retire earlier than planned, 2 March 1994

I get the feeling that there are certain people who want me to fail, and
for the life of me I don't understand why.
GRAHAM TAYLOR, England football manager, 1992

He is the first manager to go into the job realizing it is as much about
Press Conferences as matches. Much good has it done him.
DAVID LACEY, sportswriter, on Graham Taylor, after England's
loss to Holland, *Guardian*, October 1993

. . . you knock 'em down, I've got to pick them up again.
BOBBY ROBSON's frequent response to media critics of his team

Giving the England job to someone who is to the finer arts of international football what chopsticks is to Chopin would hardly conform
with the FA's ideas for improving techniques at schools level. It would
be like the next President of the Royal Academy arriving with a paint
roller.
DAVID LACEY, on possibility of Jack Charlton taking over as
England manager, *Guardian*, 1993

As soon as it dawned on me that we were short of players that combined skill and commitment, I should have forgotten about trying to
play more controlled, attractive football and settled for a real bastard
of a team.
DON REVIE (1927–89), England football manager

You need to be at least 45 to do this job. You need a lot of experience.
BILLY BINGHAM, Northern Ireland manager, October 1993

Jack is not Irish. He might own a little farm in Ireland but that doesn't make him Irish.
BILLY BINGHAM on Eire manager, Jack Charlton, October 1993

Swedes 2, Turnips 1.
Sun headline after England's exit from the European soccer championships through defeat by host nation Sweden, June 1992

Spanish 1, Onions 0.
Sun headline after England's loss to Spain in friendly international, September 1992

I'm beginning to wonder what bloody vegetable grows in Norway.
GRAHAM TAYLOR, England manager, at Press Conference after above headline and looking ahead to next game against Norway, 1993

I do everything I can to help England but I won't help to the detriment of Arsenal.
GEORGE GRAHAM, football manager, 1993

It's been the usual England get-together – everything in place except the players.
GRAHAM TAYLOR, England manager, with only 14 players out of a squad of 26, May 1993

At the moment it's a bloody horrible job. I don't want it to turn me into a horrible person.
GRAHAM TAYLOR, September 1993

I went to a school that had the motto 'Be Strong'. That's a bloody good motto. That's what I'll continue to be.
GRAHAM TAYLOR, September 1993

Norse Manure.

You've gone and dung it again, Taylor.
Sun headlines, over colour picture of manure, after World Cup defeat by Norway, 4 June 1993

Who's dung the worst job for England?
Sun front page headline, inviting readers to vote for either Graham Taylor or Prime Minister John Major, MP, 4 June 1993

Yanks 2, Planks 0.
Sun headline after England's defeat by USA, 10 June 1993

You don't look for excuses and for other people to help you. I've got to get my head down and work. I've been brought up that way. That's the only way to sort it out when you're not getting the rub of the green. It would be impossible to be at a lower point – but I went into the job with my eyes open.

You can't keep apologizing. That is a result that is in the history books now. It will probably haunt me like it haunted Walter Winterbottom when he lost to the USA in 1950.
GRAHAM TAYLOR, after defeat by USA, 10 June 1993

Everyone's got the hump with us but we're not losing on purpose. The boss is trying to do his best and pick the best side and we owe it to him to be positive.
IAN WRIGHT, England footballer, same day

Since I joined the squad we've all backed him – and I don't sense from any of the lads that anything has changed. It was as big a disappointment for us to lose to America as it was for the manager and everyone in England. But we are behind the boss 100 per cent and we'll be trying to rectify the position against Brazil.
PAUL INCE, then acting England captain, 11 June 1993

The Boston Dangler. Taylor is hanging on. You can finish him off.
The *Sun* urging fans to write to the FA Chairman, Sir Bert Millichip, demanding that Taylor be sacked, June 1993

His critics closed in for the kill. They could smell blood.
HARRY HARRIS, *Daily Mirror*, after England's defeat by USA, June 1993

My one and only policy is to hold a referendum on the England managership.
PETER NEWMAN standing for the 'Sack Graham Taylor Party' in the Christchurch by-election, July 1993

It's about reigning almost as a king but not being able to govern.
GRAHAM TAYLOR about the England manager's job, just before his last game v. San Marino, November 1993

Everyone should sit tight, stay quiet and get behind the manager with our fingers crossed in the hope that we get there.

Graham has handled the whole job well. But he hasn't got as many World Cup points as we would like.

How many clubs, hand on heart, can say they've done everything possible to help England's cause?
GRAHAM KELLY, Football Association Chief Executive, November 1993

Free market policies have ruined our national economy. Now they threaten our national game. Increased commercial pressures have led to too many games, a 'winning at all costs' mentality, numerous injuries and massive transfer inflation spirals.
DAN CURRY, Report for Institute for Public Policy Research, 1993

Pumpkins don't really turn into golden coaches, or turnips into victorious managers of the England football team. ... Graham Taylor and Lawrie McMenemy ... yesterday did the expected and dignified thing. They quit. ... It is an expected and solemn moment. They will not be there to kick around any longer. The world will pause awhile for a second; a few relatively benign things may be written about the departed regime; and then it will be visceral business as usual, building up Graham Taylor's successor as wonder man, then pulling him to pieces. That's a very English ritual ...
The Times leader, November 1993

Who on earth would want a job like this?
The Times leader

That's your allotment.
Sun headline after Graham Taylor's resignation, December 1993

I saw Graham Taylor on the touchline when England were playing Holland. Terrible sight, he was: white faced and desperate. I really felt for the man. Now we're told that the best people don't want his job. They don't want their families messed up and they don't want their lives pulled apart by people who don't know and don't care. And I understand that . . .
GRAHAM GOOCH, English cricketer, December 1993

Well, maybe Graham Taylor should have done something to stop all that nonsense. He should have been strong enough to take a stand at the outset, instead of letting the papers get away with it. I don't think Alf Ramsey would have stood for anything like that, he set his stall out early and refused to budge.
BOBBY CHARLTON, English footballer, on the media criticism of Taylor, December 1993

It's a true world game now, and we are a small, island nation. We will not be greatly missed in America for the very reason we failed to qualify. There are many better teams making the trip. There are no duck-egg teams any more. It's no disgrace to miss out.
BOBBY CHARLTON, December 1993

The only people who really know what the job of England manager is like, and what is required, are the people who have done it; Walter Winterbottom, Alf Ramsey, Ron Greenwood, Graham Taylor and me.
BOBBY ROBSON, former England manager, December 1993

You've got to be joking. Even the Pope would have second thoughts.
ROY HODGSON, Switzerland manager, when asked if he would apply for the England job, 1993

I looked forward to the last World Cup in Italy but I didn't know then what I was letting myself in for. Now I do – and I know it'll be questions, video cameras and high profile all the time. There's no fun in that for me. The enjoyment is all for the fans and that's something at least I'm glad about.
JACK CHARLTON, Eire manager, December 1993

I had my ears checked at a clinic in Dublin and the doctors gave me a brain scan at the same time. There was nothing in it.
JACK CHARLTON, March 1994

As manager of the national team, you know that, apart from the Chancellor, you will probably be the most hated man in the country.
OSVALDO ARDILES, West Bromwich Albion manager, disclaiming any interest in the England manager's post, 1993

A very thick skin.
A. C. SMITH, chief executive Test and County Cricket Board, asked about the qualities required in Ted Dexter's successor as Chairman of the England cricket committee, 1993

Bombay potatoes.
Sun headline after England's Test cricket defeat at Bombay, 1993

A load of Lankas.
Sun headline after England's cricket defeat by Sri Lanka, 1993

There was an awful lot of pressure. I think he had just had enough. Things like this can affect your whole family. I'm lucky. My wife, Sue, is very strong and she can take it. But it is now the way of things in cricket that if the England team is doing badly, there have to be heads put on the block and people don't mind how it is done.
KEITH FLETCHER, England cricket manager, commenting on resignation of Ted Dexter, August 1993

The fact is that it would not have made the slightest difference this summer, whoever had been in charge. We have not got the quality and experience of players that the Australians have. On top of that, we have performed 20 per cent below par and Australia, to their great credit, 20 per cent above par. There's the difference.
KEITH FLETCHER, August 1993

The name that kept cropping up ... was that of M. J. K. Smith ... who captained England twenty-five times in the sixties, who has no apparent pressing business commitments, might be able to manage the tour to the West Indies this winter and has not made an obvious prat of himself in public in recent memory.
MATTHEW ENGEL, *Guardian*, on successors to Dexter, August 1993

Welcome, MJK, to the war zone.
The *Guardian* comment, December 1993

Football managers get too much credit and too much of the blame.
ALF RAMSEY, former England football manager

One of the main reasons I never became England manager was because the FA thought I would take over and run the show. They were dead right.
BRIAN CLOUGH, football manager

It [the media] seems to me to have nothing to do with the job I'm supposed to do. It's absolutely incidental.

I'm sure if I read it, it would hurt me. But I don't read it.
TED DEXTER, Chairman of the Cricket Selection Committee, on the effect of the media pressures, June 1993

Just make sure you don't lose.
GRAHAM TAYLOR's advice to his successor as England manager, Terry Venables, February 1994

Do I not like that.
GRAHAM TAYLOR, England manager, watching Poland break away against England in World Cup qualifier 1993 (as heard on *Cutting Edge* TV documentary)

Index

INDEX BY NAME

INDEX BY SUBJECT